This publication has been made
possible by a generous grant from the
PROVIDENT NATIONAL BANK
PHILADELPHIA

Philadelphia:

Three Centuries of

SELECTIONS FROM THE BICENTENNIAL EXHIBITION HELD AT THE

American Art

PHILADELPHIA MUSEUM OF ART FROM APRIL 11 TO OCTOBER 10, 1976

PHILADELPHIA MUSEUM OF ART   1976

Foreword

Among the great powers of the world, the United States is a very young nation. The country as we know it has developed in only three hundred years, and it is but two centuries since the signing of the Declaration of Independence. In early July 1776, when that brave document proclaiming the rights of those living in the Colonies as well as their independence from George III was read from the steps of what today we call Independence Hall, Philadelphia was a major city of the British Empire. Indeed, it was the fourth largest city in the English-speaking world—a center of trade and of learning. Its houses were solidly built of brick and extended along regularly laid out streets. The work of its many craftsmen was without equal in the Colonies. Great trading ships—importing fine objects to satisfy the sophisticated needs of householders, bringing new settlers hopeful for the promise of the new land—called at its bustling port. Understandably, its people were proud of all that had been accomplished in less than one hundred years; proud, and deeply resolved that their rights should be respected.

Philadelphia was briefly the capital of the United States; for a longer period it was the core of America's financial world; and the city has remained a major cosmopolitan center. During the two centuries of the nation's independence, Philadelphia has grown greatly in its size and population; it has been immeasurably enriched by successive waves of newcomers emigrating from different parts of the world; and the fine tradition of its arts has continued to the present.

A vivid impression of the way of life of Philadelphia's successive generations may be gained by a thoughtful consideration of the buildings they erected, the objects they chose for daily use, the pictures and sculptures that decorated their houses and the city's public places. With the exception of New York, and possibly of Boston, no other city in the United States has had such a brilliant history of constant creativity.

This exhibition has been created to present the breadth and the quality of the arts of this city from its founding to the present. In visiting the exhibition, much is to be learned about Philadelphia; but, even more important, the method of such a considered study of this community's achievement may successfully be applied to every city or town in this country in order to foster a better understanding of those whose commitment has made each center what it is today. Indeed, such a thoughtful assessment of the past is the soundest basis for creating a responsible future.

This exhibition has been possible only because of the dedicated efforts of a considerable group of scholars; their understanding of Philadelphia's achievement has developed through studying the documents of the past and communicating with artists and craftsmen today. The much more elaborate, complete catalogue of the exhibition presents in great detail the results of their research. This volume, deliberately designed in a more casual fashion to complement the academic method of the scholarly publication, suggests the delights awaiting every visitor as he wanders through the exhibition. It is hoped that the frequent light-hearted touch evident in the juxtaposition of the illustrations will reveal new dimensions of understanding as the book's freewheeling approach demonstrates the vitality of the city that created such a variety of fascinating objects.

The pride in the American achievement that in 1876 nurtured the construction in West Fairmount Park of the first great international exposition held on this continent and persuaded a group of Philadelphians to create this art museum has today been the basis for the decision to undertake this exhibition. Many have made it possible. The City of Philadelphia constructed new 14,000 square foot Special Exhibition Galleries, thereby completing after fifty years of dedicated effort the construction of our Museum on Fairmount. Handsome grants from the National Endowment for the Arts and from the Atlantic Richfield Foundation have assured the creation of the exhibition and its catalogue; while a grant from the Provident National Bank has funded this particular publication. Finally, more than two hundred lenders have agreed to let the Museum exhibit their treasures for as considerable a period as six months. Because of such impressive cooperation every Bicentennial visitor to the city is given the opportunity to delight in and learn from Philadelphia's remarkable contribution to the richness of the arts in the United States.

Evan H. Turner
Director

Lenders to the Exhibition

Seymour Adelman, Philadelphia

Alessandra Gallery, New York

Brooke Alexander, Inc., New York

Mrs. Raymond Pace Alexander, Philadelphia

American Antiquarian Society, Worcester, Massachusetts

American Philosophical Society, Philadelphia

American Telephone & Telegraph Co., New York

Dr. and Mrs. Morton Amsterdam, Bala Cynwyd, Pennsylvania

Anonymous (36)

Arch Street Presbyterian Church, Philadelphia

Arnot Art Museum, Elmira, New York

The Art Institute of Chicago

The Athenaeum of Philadelphia

Atwater Kent Museum, Philadelphia

Laurence Bach, Philadelphia

The Baltimore Museum of Art

Katharine Beale Barclay, Wynnewood, Pennsylvania

The Barra Foundation, Inc., Philadelphia

Anne Chew Barringer, Radnor, Pennsylvania

Richard W. Barringer, Jr., Haverford, Pennsylvania

Mr. and Mrs. James Biddle, Andalusia, Pennsylvania

Morris Blackburn, Philadelphia

Estate of Barbara Blondeau

Mr. and Mrs. Joseph Bobrowicz, Philadelphia

Gerald Bordman, Philadelphia

Luther W. Brady, Philadelphia

The Brooklyn Museum, New York

Mr. and Mrs. T. Wistar Brown, 4th, Ardmore, Pennsylvania

Mrs. Charles L. Bybee, Houston, Texas

Edward J. Byrne Studio, Doylestown, Pennsylvania

Mr. and Mrs. Henry Cadwalader, York Harbor, Maine

Captain John Cadwalader, USNR (Ret.), Blue Bell, Pennsylvania

Margaretta Oliver Caesar, Evergreen, Colorado

The Campbell House Museum, St. Louis, Missouri

The Carpenters' Company of the City and County of Philadelphia

John B. Carson, M.D., Newtown Square, Pennsylvania

Mrs. Gardner Cassatt, Bryn Mawr, Pennsylvania

Mrs. Alfred D. Chandler, Wilmington, Delaware

Chester County Historical Society, West Chester, Pennsylvania

Christ Church, Philadelphia

Eleanor and Van Deren Coke, Albuquerque, New Mexico

Mr. and Mrs. Bertram D. Coleman, Bryn Mawr, Pennsylvania

Colonial Williamsburg Foundation, Williamsburg, Virginia

The Columbus (Ohio) Gallery of Fine Arts

Sophie Chandler Consagra, Wilmington, Delaware

The Corning Museum of Glass, Corning, New York

Francis James Dallett, Villanova, Pennsylvania

Thomas L. Davies, Berwyn, Pennsylvania

Mr. and Mrs. Leonard Davis, New York

Delaware Art Museum, Wilmington

The Detroit Institute of Arts

Mr. and Mrs. H. Richard Dietrich, Jr., Chester Springs, Pennsylvania

Dietrich Corporation, Reading, Pennsylvania

Charlotte Dobrasin, Philadelphia

Drexel Museum Collection, Drexel University, Philadelphia

Helen Williams Drutt, Philadelphia

Helen Drutt Gallery, Philadelphia

Miss Edith Emerson, Philadelphia

Woodruff Jones Emlen, Bryn Mawr, Pennsylvania

The Episcopal Academy, Merion, Pennsylvania

Walter Erlebacher, Elkins Park, Pennsylvania

The Wharton Esherick Museum, Paoli, Pennsylvania

Charles C. Fahlen, Philadelphia

National Portrait Gallery, Smithsonian Institution, Washington, D.C.

The National Trust for Historic Preservation—Cliveden

Nelson Gallery—Atkins Museum, Kansas City, Missouri

The Newark Museum, Newark, New Jersey

The New-York Historical Society

Dr. and Mrs. Perry Ottenberg, Merion, Pennsylvania

Pennsylvania Academy of the Fine Arts, Philadelphia

Philadelphia City Archives

The Philadelphia College of Art

Philadelphia Gun Club

The Philadelphia Saving Fund Society

Marie Merkel Pollard, Dallas, Texas

Lydia Bond Powel, Stonington, Connecticut

Provident National Bank Collection, Philadelphia

Reading Company, Philadelphia

Mr. and Mrs. David P. Redfield, Doylestown, Pennsylvania

Lola S. Reed, M.D., Phoenixville, Pennsylvania

Arthur Robinson, Harrison, New York

Abby Aldrich Rockefeller Folk Art Collection, Williamsburg, Virginia

Dr. Stanley W. Roman, New York

Rosedown Plantation, St. Francisville, Louisiana

Charles Rudy, Ottsville, Pennsylvania

The St. Louis Art Museum

Sagamore Hill National Historic Site—National Park Service, Oyster Bay, New York

Gordon K. Saltar, Arden, Delaware

San Antonio Art League, San Antonio, Texas

Dr. and Mrs. Ira Leo Schamberg, Jenkintown, Pennsylvania

Schweitzer Gallery, New York

Estate of Howell Lewis Shay

Phillips Simkin, Philadelphia

Judy Skoogfors, Philadelphia

Leif Skoogfors, New York

E. Newbold Smith, Paoli, Pennsylvania

Edward Wanton Smith, Jr., Darien, Connecticut

Joseph Sorger, Philadelphia

Dr. Isaac Starr, Philadelphia

Mrs. Samuel S. Starr, Media, Pennsylvania

Mr. and Mrs. Anthony A. P. Stuempfig, Philadelphia

Charles V. Swain, Doylestown, Pennsylvania

Mr. and Mrs. Joseph Tanenbaum, Bayside, New York

David Beckwith Taylor, Jr., Leland, Mississippi

Dr. Edward Teitelman, Camden, New Jersey

Mr. and Mrs. George E. Thomas, Philadelphia

Trump and Company, Flourtown, Pennsylvania

Mrs. Andrew Van Pelt, Radnor, Pennsylvania

George Vaux, ARPS, Bryn Mawr, Pennsylvania

Venturi and Rauch, Architects and Planners, Philadelphia

Peggy Macdowell Walters, Roanoke, Virginia

Washington County Museum of Fine Arts, Hagerstown, Maryland

Mr. and Mrs. Samuel Ward, Moylan, Pennsylvania

Webster, Inc., Fine Art, Chevy Chase, Maryland

The Westmoreland County Museum of Art, Greensburg, Pennsylvania

Richard T. Wharton, Stamford, Connecticut

Mrs. Thomas Raeburn White, Philadelphia

Mrs. Jacob H. Whitebook, Elkins Park, Pennsylvania

Whitney Museum of American Art, New York

Robert M. Winokur, Horsham, Pennsylvania

The Henry Francis du Pont Winterthur Museum, Winterthur, Delaware

Dr. and Mrs. Melvyn D. Wolf, Flint, Michigan

The Naomi Wood Collection, Woodford Mansion, East Fairmount Park, Philadelphia

Yale University Art Gallery, New Haven

Harvey Z. Yellin—Samuel Yellin Collection, Philadelphia

Editor's Note

This is a Bicentennial publication of the Philadelphia Museum of Art, issued on the occasion of the exhibition *Philadelphia: Three Centuries of American Art* and supported by a generous grant from the Provident National Bank. In conceiving this project, the Museum and the Bank wished to make available to our numerous visitors a publication that would be both an introduction to this exhibition and a handsome reminder of their visit to the Philadelphia Museum of Art.

Our method of presentation is familiar, a journalistic survey of the exhibition through a series of bold illustrations. In choosing and arranging the plates, our first goal has been to lay before the reader a succession of strong images not unlike the visual memories one might expect to take home from a visit to an exhibition of this scale and diversity. Certain themes have emerged during the process of selection—Philadelphia's fine craftsmanship, the academic tradition, depiction of the human figure and of nature, representation of the city, patriotic motifs—but in the organization of the book, these themes have been purposely made to overlap. Above all, it is the visual impact of the objects rather than their thematic or historical significance that has guided us.

The chronological sequence of the objects as displayed in the galleries has been discarded here, and no attempt has been made to provide a complete record or to present a didactic survey of the exhibition. That is left to the extensive, fully illustrated catalogue, published simultaneously. Likewise, we mean to draw no broad conclusions about the arts of Philadelphia from the accompanying captions, which are intended to provide introductions only to the works reproduced on these pages. In preparing these texts, we have drawn upon the material in the exhibition catalogue, and the reader is directed there for additional information and full documentation on each object. The authors of those catalogue texts are Robin Bolton-Smith, John Caldwell, Patricia A. Chapin, Carol Clark, Phillip H. Curtis, Anne d'Harnoncourt, Sandra Downie, Dorinda Evans, Donald L. Fennimore, Kathleen Foster, Beatrice B. Garvan, Frederick Gutheim, David A. Hanks, Kathryn B. Hiesinger, Christine A. Jackson, Ellen S. Jacobowitz, Ruth Fine Lehrer, Lynne A. Leopold, Gordon Marshall, Elsie S. McGarvey, Susanna K. Morikawa, Stephanie A. Munsing, David Orr, Peter J. Parker, Ann B. Percy, Bernard Reilly, Joseph Rishel, Abigail Schade, Darrel L. Sewell, Theodor Siegl, William F. Stapp, Page Talbott, George Thomas, D. Dodge Thompson, Richard Webster, Kenneth M. Wilson, and Caroline P. Wistar.

George H. Marcus

Gas-Jet Eagle
About 1848
Iron, length 100″
(254 cm)
Atwater Kent Museum,
Philadelphia
Catalogue no. 284

Raphaelle Peale (1774-1825)
After the Bath
1823
Oil on canvas, 29 x 24"
(73.7 x 61 cm)
Nelson Gallery-Atkins
Museum, Kansas City.
Nelson Fund
Catalogue no. 214

Raphaelle Peale created *After the Bath* to tease his nagging wife into thinking he had hidden a painting of a female nude under one of her best napkins, seemingly just laundered and hung in front of his canvas with straight pins. He triumphed when she raced to his easel to pull it off but found herself scratching at a painting instead, thus proving he had greater ability than she had ever given him credit for.

Raphaelle Peale was one of four artist sons of Charles Willson Peale, the best-known of Philadelphia's eighteenth-century painters. The artistic emphasis in the Peale family was on accuracy of representation, which led inevitably to experimentation with "deceptions," paintings adroitly created to fool and astound the viewer. The striking success of this painting as a piece of visual trickery is due chiefly to the sharp contrast between the very tangible, meticulously painted cloth in the foreground and the hazy figure scarcely visible behind it: since the cloth appears so real, the figure must be painted; and if the figure is painted, then the cloth must be real. Surely the most extraordinary bit of deception in American art, *After the Bath* is considered Raphaelle Peale's masterpiece, both for its spare abstract design and its clever, deftly rendered illusion.

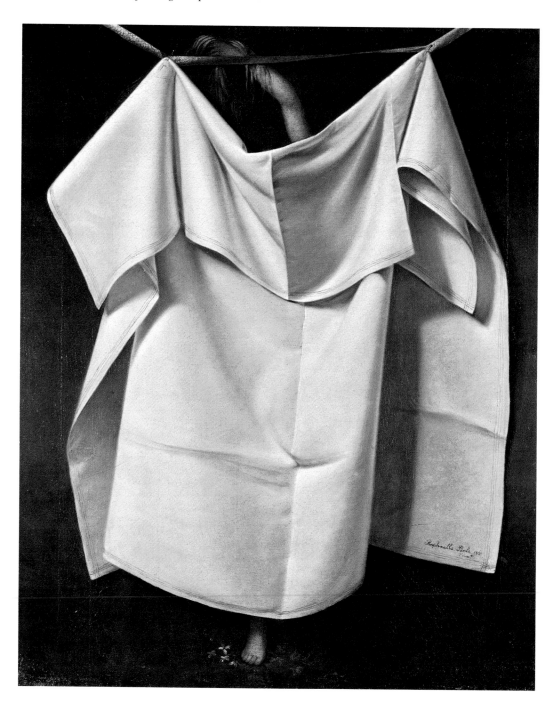

William Harnett
(1848–1892)
The Artist's Card Rack
1879
Oil on canvas, 30 x 25″
(76.2 x 63.5 cm)
The Metropolitan
Museum of Art, New
York. Morris K. Jesup
Fund, 1966
Catalogue no. 353

Considered little more than a trickster and a clever craftsman by many critics during his relatively brief career, William Harnett was nonetheless very popular with the general public. Continuing the tradition of "deceptions" initiated in Philadelphia a century earlier by the Peale family, Harnett painted for a popular audience that was captivated by the surpassing technical skill necessary to imitate nature so closely that the eye would be fooled. In such paintings as *The Artist's Card Rack* he was able to achieve his most convincing illusions. The loop of string and the various letters and calling cards inserted into the makeshift tape rack tacked on a door all cast highly illusory shadows (especially the fragmentary nailed card, which before being torn had shielded the area behind it from darkening like the rest of the wooden surface). The pictorial logic of this seemingly random but indeed carefully calculated clutter heightens the effect of the deception.

Most likely this picture was painted on commission from its first owner, Israel Reifsnyder, a wool merchant, who is perhaps referred to by the word "Snyde" written on the wall below the rack. If the other words, addresses, and scrawls have any specific meanings, these are yet to be deciphered, and the newspaper clipping, so meticulously rendered that it seems as if it must easily be readable, is totally illegible—a final perverse triumph of the illusionist's art.

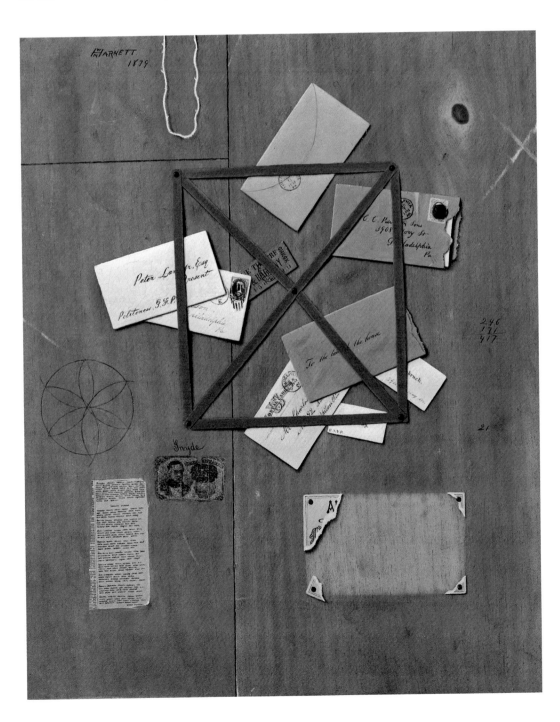

Armchair
1725–50
Painted maple and
hickory with rush seat,
height 44¾″ (113.7 cm)
Philadelphia Museum of
Art. Given by Titus C.
Geesey. 69-284-14
Catalogue no. 24

Slat-back chairs were probably already being made in Philadelphia by 1700, since soon after, their manufacture and sale were recorded in many ledgers and account books. The graceful arched shape of the slats was a Delaware Valley feature, and the chair's comfort was enhanced by the concave curve given the slats by a special device, the slat press. A draw knife honed the slats into their flexible thinness; mortising chisels fitted them into their slots in the back posts; braces and bits drilled holes for stretchers and seat rails; leather-padded hammers pounded the chair together; and the final weaving of the rush seat secured all parts. Slat-back chairs were generally made of maple and came in a variety of sizes, styles, and colors. Presumably, over the years, they were painted, repainted, repaired, and repainted again. This chair has had several coats of paint, and at least two, Venetian red and Spanish brown, are evident.

William L. Price
(1861–1916)
Reclining Armchair
Made by John Maene
1901–9
Oak, height 46″ (116.8
cm)
Mr. and Mrs. Samuel
Ward, Moylan,
Pennsylvania
Catalogue no. 398

The strong, straight lines and unornamented surfaces of this oak armchair, emphasizing the natural wood grain, signify a return to simple forms and handcrafted construction that came into vogue late in the nineteenth century. Of comfortable proportions, the chair, which would have been used with cushions, adjusts to several reclining positions by means of a ratchet. Designed by the architect William L. Price in a form derived from the famous English "Morris" chair, it was produced by the craftsman John Maene in the workshop of Price's Rose Valley community near Philadelphia.

Charles Demuth
(1883–1935)
*In Vaudeville (Dancer
with Chorus)*
1918
Watercolor on paper,
12¾ x 8″ (32.4 x 20.3 cm)
Philadelphia Museum of
Art. A.E. Gallatin
Collection. 52-61-18
Catalogue no. 434 b

Charles Demuth was fascinated by the hectic,
colorful, and often decadent nightlife of the
entertainment world. Though he frequented the
music halls and bohemian dives of New York in the
years during and immediately after World War I, he
found picturesque material for his art close to home
as well, at vaudeville shows in his native Lancaster,
Pennsylvania. One can imagine him leaving the
local variety theater and strolling back to his quiet
second-floor studio overlooking the garden of the
family home in Lancaster, there to produce his
strangely disturbing images of attenuated, supple
figures in evening dress cavorting onstage within a
succession of curved forms suggested by the glare of
spotlights. His nervous, undulating line and
luminous tones are a perfect vehicle for these
disquieting nocturnal visions.

Franklin Watkins
(1894–1972)
The Fire Eater
1933–34
Oil on canvas, 60¾ x 39"
(54.2 x 99 cm)
Philadelphia Museum of
Art. Given by
twenty-eight donors.
35-46-1
Catalogue no. 461

Inspired by the animated description of a
"fire-eater," a side-show performer on Philadelphia's
South Street, Franklin Watkins created this colorful,
almost visionary interpretation of the carnival
scene. Drawn solely from the artist's imagination,
the elongated fire swallower, straining upward and
oddly foreshortened, cuts a heroic figure as he
towers over his motley audience. Despite the
fairground sketched in the distance, the vague
setting of a wooden platform and fence under a
turbulent sky suggests no specific time or place.
Watkins himself revealed one aspect of this
imagined scene which intrigued him: "I believe I
sort of thought of something difficult, perhaps
painful, being done with the people who stood about
gawking—kidding—indifferent."

William P. Daley (born
1925)
Drawing for Floor Pot
1974
Ink on paper, 11 x 8½"
(28 x 21.5 cm)
Norman and Margaret
Krecke, Philadelphia
Catalogue no. 529 b

William Daley's angular ceramic vessels are built up
of a number of hard and precise planar surfaces.
They are carefully thought out before, and
reconsidered during, their execution, through a
number of masterful detailed drawings. This study,
made after he had begun to work on the pot,
conveys a sense of monumentality well beyond the
actual scale of the piece, which is only eighteen
inches high. Much like an architect's sketches,
Daley's drawings often show the form of his pots
from more than one angle as well as the special
patterns, templates, and supports required for their
construction.

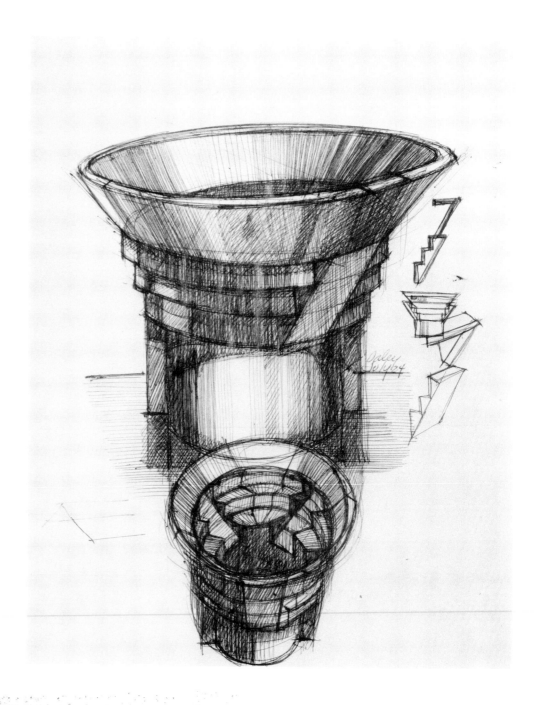

John Haviland
(1792–1852)
*Eastern State
Penitentiary (Cherry
Hill)*
Fairmount Avenue,
between Corinthian and
Twenty-second streets
1822–36
Coursed granite ashlar
Catalogue no. 215

Represented by:
*The State Penitentiary,
for the Eastern District
of Pennsylvania*
1855
From the *Pennsylvania
Journal of Prison
Discipline*, April 1856
Lithograph, 6³/₁₆ x 9⁷/₁₆"
(15.7 x 24 cm)
The Free Library of
Philadelphia

In 1829 the Boston Prison Discipline Society contended that "there is such a thing as architecture adapted to morals; that other things being equal, the prospect of improvement, in morals, depends in some degree, upon the construction of buildings." At this time, the Commonwealth of Pennsylvania, acting on the same premise, was moving prisoners into the partially completed Eastern State Penitentiary. This prison was designed as part of the "Pennsylvania System," a penal reform advocating the separation of prisoners from the influences that bred their unlawful behavior. This required not just incarceration but also isolation from fellow inmates. The prisoner was to communicate only with his conscience and the Bible left in his cell, and occupy himself working at a simple craft, such as weaving or shoemaking.

The distinctive feature of the new Eastern State Penitentiary was its radial plan, the distribution of seven cell blocks around a central rotunda like spokes from the hub of a wheel. The rotunda served as a surveillance center, and each block comprised a series of eight-by-ten-foot cells, arranged on each side of a central corridor and opening onto slightly larger, high-walled private exercise yards. The prison's radial plan was not unique—it had been executed abroad earlier on a smaller scale for jails and insane asylums—but its architect John Haviland carried the concept to its fullest realization and his name has since been associated with this concept as it has been adopted for prisons around the world.

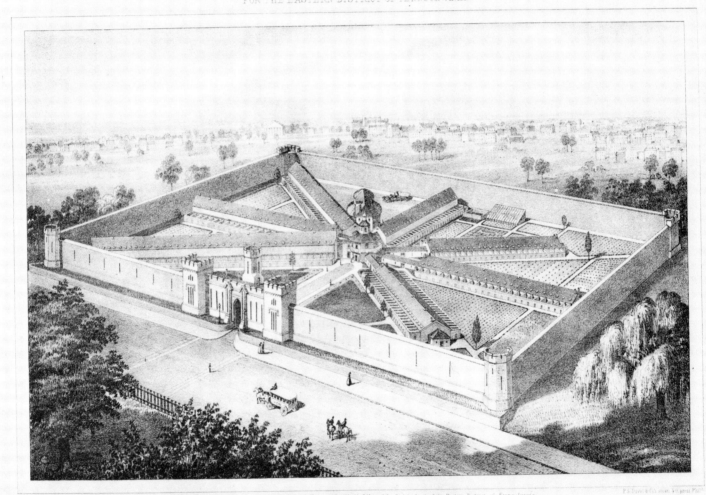

THE STATE PENITENTIARY,
FOR THE EASTERN DISTRICT OF PENNSYLVANIA.

This Institution known as "Cherry Hill State Prison" at Philadelphia, is the Model Prison of "The Pennsylvania System of Prison Discipline" or "Separate System" as it is called to distinguish it from "The Congregate". Each Convict occupies a single Cell or Workshop, and is thus separated from all other convicts. The Building was begun in 1822. The walls 30 f.t high, 12 f.t thick at base, 2f.t 9 in: at top, enclose a square plot of Ten Acres. There are 7 Corridors of Cells, capable of receiving 500 convicts. The average number confined annually is less than 300. Some cells are 11 f.t 9 in. by 7 f.t 6 in. with yards attached, 15 f.t by 8 f.t. Others are double this size, all lighted and warmed and ventilated. Gas is introduced into the corridors. Heat by hot water thro' pipes. Water in each cell and other Conveniences.
The above is a Bird's Eye View of the Buildings, Grounds and Environs.

Philip Syng, Jr.
(1703–1789)
Coffeepot
About 1753
Silver, height 11⅞"
(30.2 cm)
Philadelphia Museum of
Art. Purchased: John D.
McIlhenny Fund. 66-20-1
Catalogue no. 44

Tea and coffee, introduced into America during the late seventeenth century, rapidly grew in popularity. The preparation and consumption of these beverages required new equipment, teacups and coffee cups, tea caddies, and tea urns, as well as the tall coffeepot and the squat teapot, which were made in a variety of materials, among them silver, pewter, pottery, and porcelain. This coffeepot by the master silversmith Philip Syng, Jr., elaborately decorated with swirling motifs of flowers and scrolls, combines the robust basic shape favored in Philadelphia with a freely applied ornamentation derived from English models.

Syng, like many of Philadelphia's most important Colonial craftsmen, was active in all areas of city life: he was a vestryman at Christ Church, a trustee of the College of Philadelphia (University of Pennsylvania), Treasurer of Philadelphia, and a charter member of the Library Company. He also worked with Benjamin Franklin in developing the lightning rod.

Attributed to Thomas
Haig's Northern Liberty
Pottery
Coffeepot
About 1815–30
Glazed red earthenware,
height 10¾" (27.3 cm)
The Metropolitan
Museum of Art, New
York. Rogers Fund, 1922
Catalogue no. 205

This tall red-clay coffeepot, covered with a shiny glaze and ornamented only with incised bands, is distinguished for its simple, yet fashionable design. Thomas Haig was one of many Philadelphia potters producing earthenware during the early nineteenth century. They supplied the American market with pottery for everyday use that successfully competed with English and Continental imports for quality and cost. With an ample supply of raw materials, trained workers, extensive markets, and excellent transportation, Philadelphia was a major center for the production of household and industrial earthenware. The tea sets and tablewares attributed to Thomas Haig's Northern Liberty Pottery are outstanding examples of Philadelphia craftsmanship and artistic excellence. Once common, their fragility has made them rarer than similar objects made of silver during the same period.

Henry O. Tanner
(1859-1937)
Portrait of the Artist's Mother
1897
Oil on canvas, 29¼ x 39½" (74.2 x 100.3 cm)
Mrs. Raymond Pace Alexander, Philadelphia
Catalogue no. 389

In 1891, Henry O. Tanner, who had studied with Thomas Eakins at the Pennsylvania Academy of the Fine Arts, left for Paris to further his education, and continued to live there throughout his life. This portrait of his mother, completed during a trip home in 1897, is somewhat more quiet and contemplative than the scenes of family life he had painted in the 1880s and early 1890s. It shows that Tanner was well aware of the international art world, for the picture bears a striking relationship to Whistler's now famous portrait of his mother, titled *Arrangement in Gray and Black*, which was purchased by the French Government and displayed in Paris the year Tanner arrived. The same compositional elements appear in both canvases, including the drapery and framed picture in the background. While Whistler's portrait also sought to convey his devotion to his mother, he was at least equally intrigued with the formal elements of his composition, the abstract "arrangement" of subdued tones of color. Tanner, though also much concerned with this aspect as he balances, lightens, and completes his composition with the drapery that spills over the side of the chair, places his major emphasis on a warmly sympathetic portrayal of his mother.

Eva Lawrence
Watson-Schütze
(1867–1935)
Portrait Study
1904
Published in *Camera
Work*, January 1905
Photogravure, 8⅜ x 6½"
(21.4 x 16.5 cm)
Philadelphia Museum of
Art. Given by Carl
Zigrosser. 66-205-9(8)
Catalogue no. 408

Like Tanner's portrait of his mother, this picture of a seated woman is a balanced and harmonious arrangement of all its components, as caught by the camera lens. Its expressive force lies in the subtle tonal gradations of black and gray that gracefully yet distinctly outline each part of the composition. Although this photogravure consciously imitates the style of paintings of its period and reflects the influence of Whistler, the photographer has adhered to what she considered the limitations of her medium and has in no way manipulated the image during the developing or printing process. Eva Watson-Schütze, possibly a student of Thomas Eakins at the Pennsylvania Academy of the Fine Arts, was a founding member of the Photo-Secession group, and a leading exponent of photography as an independent and distinctive artistic medium. The 1905 publication of this portrait and three other photographs in the influential Photo-Secession journal *Camera Work* emphasized her stature among the leading photographic artists of her day.

Rebecca Scattergood
Savery (1770–1855)
Patchwork Quilt
1839
Cotton chintz, 119½ x
115" (303.5 x 292.1 cm)
Philadelphia Museum of
Art. Gift of Mrs. Lewis
Barton and Mrs. David
Barclay. 75-5-1
Catalogue no. 262

The craze for cotton patchwork in America, which began soon after 1800, continued in full force until about 1870. In the prevailing nineteenth-century tradition, quilting was used chiefly to reinforce the coverlet rather than to decorate it. Quilting was often accomplished at a quilting bee, a social event that occasioned the convivial gathering of a number of women and relieved the monotony of the task.

According to a note from Rebecca Savery's great granddaughter, this quilt is made up of 3,903 colorful pieces of chintz. Forming the traditional "sunburst" pattern, the diamond-shaped patches radiate in concentric octagonal rings, each of a different chintz, from a central eight-pointed "star." Not only is this quilt a superb example of the quilter's art, but the thirty-four or more distinct

fabrics to be counted in it comprise a valuable catalogue of cotton chintz fabrics available in the mid-nineteenth century.

Gillinder & Sons
(1861–1930)
Bowl
1903
Flint (lead) glass,
diameter 10″ (25.4 cm)
Philadelphia Museum of
Art. Given by Gillinder
& Sons. 04-2
Catalogue no. 402

The intricate style of cutting glass that allowed the deep-cut, dense patterns to obscure almost the entire original surface of this bowl was popular during what is known as the "brilliant period," from about 1885 to 1915. It was made possible by improvements in furnace design, glass chemistry, and melting practices that yielded the high-quality, thick lead-glass blanks which, when cut with these allover patterns, produced the brilliant refraction that gave this style of cut glass its name. Cut glass, which has only lately returned to favor among collectors, has always been costly because of the labor involved in producing it. Each separate part of the pattern must undergo five distinct and painstaking operations of cutting, smoothing, and polishing.

Joseph Breintnall (died 1746)
Nature Prints of Leaves
1731-42
Printer's ink on half sheets of paper, 12³/₁₆ x 15³/₈" (31 x 39 cm)
The Library Company of Philadelphia
Catalogue no. 29

Of all the "books" printed in Philadelphia, none is quite so unique as Joseph Breintnall's two volumes of leaf prints. The volumes comprise a group of loose sheets printed with delicate impressions of leaves, and sometimes feathers and cloth, on one or both sides of a sheet. Breintnall's method of printing was comparatively simple. Obtaining specimens from William Bartram's renowned garden, or from his own travels, he inked both sides of a leaf, placed it between a folded sheet of paper, and pulled it through a printing press. He experimented with different methods of inking the leaves, using first a roller and then alternating the roller with a standard printer's leather ball. Later he had a velvet inking ball made, which produced his best prints, showing the minutest details of the smallest leaf, feather, or cloth sample.

Breintnall quickly learned that no single method of preparing the leaves sufficed for all species. Small, veined, or delicate specimens had to be printed when freshly picked or, if dried, resoaked in water to make them less brittle. Large, sappy leaves had first to be dried, usually under piles of newspaper or between the pages of a book, and then lightly moistened with water and blotted before being finally inked. Breintnall is known to have dried one particularly soft and fleshy leaf for eight years before he felt it was ready for taking a print.

Benjamin Smith Barton
(1766–1815)
Rattlesnake Skeleton
About 1805
Pen and ink, brush and
wash on paper; 14¾ x
39⅜" (37.5 x 101.5 cm)
American Philosophical
Society, Philadelphia
Catalogue no. 163

The naturalist Benjamin Smith Barton had been interested in snakes long before he produced this remarkable drawing of a rattlesnake skeleton about 1805. In 1796 he published *A Memoir Concerning the Fascinating Faculty which Has Been Ascribed to the Rattle-snake. . . .* In this essay he refuted the then widely held belief that the rattlesnake was capable of so enticing birds and other small animals that they offered themselves as its victims. Forthrightly contradicting the most eminent European scientists, Barton proved by a combination of empirical experiment and close observation of snakes in their natural surroundings that they had no such power. He concluded that observers had probably been misled by what were actually frantic efforts of female birds to protect their young. Despite these investigations, Barton confessed he was so repelled by snakes that he was unable to begin a long-contemplated series of experiments involving "slowly and cautiously dissecting and examining their structure and their function." Eventually, he appears to have overcome his revulsion, for this drawing is part of a series of anatomical studies of the rattlesnake that Barton probably did as illustrations for his planned, but never published, treatise on "The Anatomy and Physiology of the Rattlesnake." Whatever its connection with Barton's scientific investigations, *Rattlesnake Skeleton* is itself a remarkable object. The beautifully precise strokes of Barton's pen reveal the skeleton as a structure of formal, almost abstract grace. This quality, together with its stark placement on a large, otherwise bare sheet, makes the drawing a significant artistic expression that in a sense foreshadows twentieth-century work by Georgia O'Keeffe.

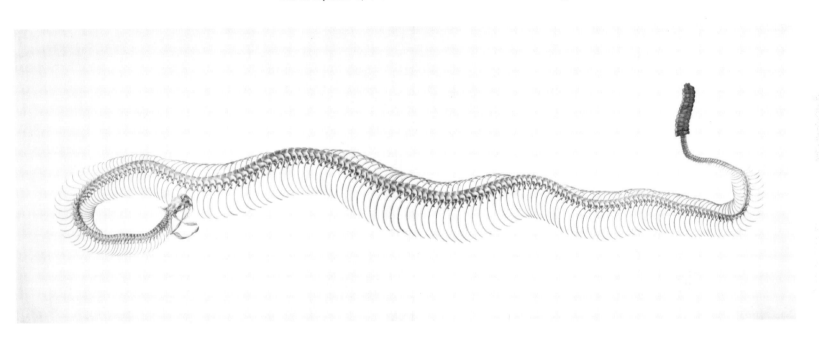

Morton Schamberg
(1881–1918)
God
About 1917
Wooden miter box and
cast-iron plumbing trap,
height 10½" (26.7 cm)
Philadelphia Museum of
Art. The Louise and
Walter Arensberg
Collection. 50-134-182
Catalogue no. 438

Morton Schamberg's only sculpture, *God*, is perhaps the most irreverent object produced in Philadelphia during the first decades of this century. The international circle of artists and writers who gathered in the New York apartment of Louise and Walter Arensberg between 1915 and 1921 was largely responsible for the controversial phenomenon of "New York Dada," and Schamberg could claim the distinction of being the sole delegate from Philadelphia. Marcel Duchamp, Man Ray, and Francis Picabia were the leaders of the new movement, which staged outrageous events, published short-lived little magazines, and produced works of art calculated to baffle, and perhaps even outrage, the public.

Little is known about the creation of this sculpture, but the juxtaposition of the plain wooden miter box with the rather gracefully curved plumbing trap is a three-dimensional notion very akin to Schamberg's precise and elegant "mechanical" paintings. The creation of a sculpture by bringing together two common, apparently incongruous elements was a bold gesture for 1917, decades ahead of its time. Schamberg made several photographic studies of *God*, with the plumbing trap set in different positions, and it seems clear he thought of the work as an abstract combination of forms as well as the expression of a Dadaist intent to shock.

H. Lyman Saÿen
(1875–1918)
The Thundershower
1917–18
Tempera and pencil on
plywood, 36 x 46"
(91.4 x 116.8 cm)
National Collection of
Fine Arts, Smithsonian
Institution, Washington,
D.C. Gift of H. Lyman
Saÿen to His Nation,
1967
Catalogue no. 440

H. Lyman Saÿen's extended exposure to the current art of Paris, where he lived from 1906 to 1914, and especially his admiration for the paintings of his teacher Henri Matisse, account for the appearance of this innovative painting style in Philadelphia by 1917. Saÿen's Parisian experiences have been mingled with his desire to create a thoroughly American modern art. In this boldly decorative, high-spirited composition, he has reduced the visible effects of a thundershower to a series of curved and jagged rhythms; amid these forms, which can be variously read as rain, lightning, and clouds, two charming young women frolic. Saÿen's fresh style is sparked with a note of humor underlined by his inscribing the title prominently on the face of the painting. It has been suggested that this was his witty response to a disgruntled reviewer who had complained that Saÿen's works were "futuristic in tendency, puzzling to the critics . . . , yet no doubt interesting if the artist could transmit a message as to his intent." Like Marcel Duchamp's lettering on his *Nude Descending a Staircase* five years earlier, Saÿen's title gives rise to as much mystery as it would appear to dispel.

THE THUNDERSHOWER
LYMAN SAÿEN

Robert Smith
(1722-1777)
Carpenters' Hall
Chestnut Street, between
Fourth Street and
Whalebone Alley
1770-71, doorway 1792
Brick and granite facade
with wood trim
Catalogue no. 85

Represented by:
Attributed to Thomas
Bedwell (active 1779-95)
after Robert Smith
*Carpenters' Hall: North
Elevation*
From *The Rules of Work
of the Carpenters'
Company of the City
and County of
Philadelphia,* 1786
Engraving, 9 x 6" (20.3 x
10.5 cm)
The Carpenters'
Company of the City and
County of Philadelphia

The Carpenters' Company was formed in 1727 "for the purpose of obtaining instruction in the science of architecture and assisting such of their members as should by accident be in need of support," but implicit in its organization was the need to oversee the quality of workmanship and dictate prices. Successive petitions had been presented to the City Council to formalize what had been customary among local carpenters, especially apprenticeship terms and contract and measuring regulations; when these failed, the carpenters organized themselves and eventually, in 1786, printed their small handbook of rules and prices for the edification and regulation of their membership. The content of this book was a trade secret, and any member who showed it to an outsider was liable to expulsion from the Company.

This engraving of the north elevation of Carpenters' Hall from the Carpenters' Company rule book was probably made from the architect's drawings expressly for the 1786 publication. Robert Smith, architect of the Christ Church steeple and St. Peter's Church, is given credit for the design of Carpenters' Hall, and with the exception of the doorway—completed in 1792—and the roof urns, the building stands as designed and built in 1770-71, set back from Chestnut Street, between Fourth Street and Whalebone Alley.

Frederick DeBourg
Richards (1822–1903)
*Carpenters' Court
and Hall*
1859
Salt print, 8¾ x 6″ (21.3
x 15.2 cm)
The Library Company of
Philadelphia
Catalogue no. 314 b

Carpenters' Hall, which in 1774 was the meeting place of the First Continental Congress, was one of a number of Philadelphia's historically significant public institutions and private residences photographed by Frederick Richards during the 1850s. These photographs were preserved by the antiquarian Charles A. Poulson, who perhaps commissioned Richards to record these buildings for posterity. The angle at which Richards chose to show Carpenters' Hall and the sharpness of detail throughout the photograph are striking.

John East (active
1697–1716)
Flagon
1707–8
Silver, height 11½"
(29.2 cm)
Christ Church,
Philadelphia

Philip Syng, Sr.
(1676–1739)
Flagon
1715
Silver, height 11½"
(29.2 cm)
Christ Church,
Philadelphia
Catalogue no. 14

In 1708, Queen Anne presented to Christ Church in Philadelphia three pieces of ceremonial silver—a chalice, paten, and a flagon—by the silversmith John East of London. Seven years later, with money bequeathed for the purpose, Christ Church commissioned a matching flagon from a newly arrived Irish silversmith, Philip Syng, Sr. The two tall and tapering cylindrical vessels are a pair in form, dimensions, and weight. Syng managed to duplicate the raised base, the encircling band, the grand sweep of the handle, and the cushionlike lid designed by John East. But the hingework on Syng's flagon (on the right) is not quite so precise or "finished" as that on the English model, the thumbpiece is higher, and the cast scroll ornament has softer contours compared with the concise clarity of East's flagon. Although often made for domestic use in England, the flagon became primarily a church vessel in America. Used to fill the Communion cup, or chalice, the ample flagon was a ceremonial necessity in a parish of any size.

Dress
About 1787–92
Blue silk brocade, with
white silk brocade
underdress; waist 26"
(66 cm)
Philadelphia Museum of
Art. Given by Mrs. W.
Logan MacCoy. 55-78-2
Catalogue no. 119

Dress
About 1795–99
Light-beige satin, with
quilted satin underdress;
waist 24" (60.1 cm)
Philadelphia Museum of
Art. Given by Miss Mary
Morris Boykin. 71-68-1
Catalogue no. 144

The pale-blue silk brocade dress, with its tightly
fitted bodice and three tabs accenting the waistline
on each side, was probably worn by Rebecca Hughes
of Philadelphia, who died in 1792 at age twenty-two.
Elegant in design, it is trimmed in lace and
ornamented with satin-covered buttons on the
sleeves. Another dress almost identical in cut and
with a similar underdress but more subdued in
trimming was worn by Rebecca's Quaker cousin
Mary Hollingsworth about 1795–99. Without
neglecting the precept of simplicity, Quaker clothes
often had stylish origins, though interpreted more
modestly. Some Quakers simply took the current
fashions and copied them in exquisite materials,
such as this light-beige satin, but omitted any
applied adornment.

Jonathan Shoemaker
(1726–1793)
Armchair
About 1765
Mahogany, height 39¾"
(101 cm)
Philadelphia Museum of
Art. Bequest of William
M. Doughten. 56-122-2
Catalogue no. 66

Based on models illustrated in Thomas Chippendale's *Gentleman and Cabinet-Maker's Director*, published in London in 1754, chairs of this style quickly became popular in England and the Colonies. Rectangular in outline and embellished with florid carving, the "Chippendale" chair featured shell and leaf motifs, classical fluting, and feet carved in the form of animals' paws.

This "Chippendale" armchair by Jonathan Shoemaker is distinguished for its broad and generous proportions, handsome gadrooned ropelike molding at the base of the pierced back splat, and the variety of its carved shell forms. According to an often-repeated story, a British officer quartered in Shoemaker's house during the occupation of Philadelphia in 1777 commissioned him to make a set of chairs, but the occupation was over before the set was completed and the officer left this one sample behind. Not only does this impressive armchair need no romantic story to secure its place in the arts of Philadelphia, but its style places it in the 1760s well before the beginning of the Revolution.

Ferdinand Keller
(established 1882)
Side Chair
1885-1910
Mahogany, height 41"
(104.1 cm)
Dr. and Mrs. Joseph A.
Glick, Wilmington,
Delaware
Catalogue no. 374

In the 1870s, as the Centennial celebrations approached, a new interest in the American Colonial style began to be seen in architecture and the decorative arts. However, the Centennial Exhibition of 1876 almost completely ignored this revival and no furniture in the Colonial style seems to have been shown there. In the next decade, a number of American manufacturers introduced such furniture, but the term "Colonial" was frequently used to refer to any American furniture dating from the late seventeenth century to the first quarter of the nineteenth century and the pieces produced under this name were sometimes only vaguely related to the earlier prototypes. Toward the end of the century, however, as antiquarian interest in America's early period grew, reproductions of Colonial furniture became more accurate.

This chair, manufactured by the firm of Ferdinand Keller, is a reasonably faithful copy of a Philadelphia ribbon-back "Chippendale" chair. It exhibits similar curved cresting rails, pierced intertwining back splat, and ball-and-claw feet; however, in its scale, the combination of its decorative elements and their shallow, somewhat abstracted carving, and the unusual serpentine seat front, it is clearly distinguished from the Colonial source. But the high quality of its manufacture and its faithful dependence on an original Colonial model indicate the stability of Philadelphia's keen interest in its rich heritage and a continuity of the city's fine craftsmanship.

Vest
About 1780
Embroidered and quilted
satin, center back length
23½" (59.6 cm)
Philadelphia Museum of
Art. Given by Mrs. N.
Dubois Miller.
43-17-7
Catalogue no. 111 a

Vest Pattern
1780–1800
Embroidered silk, 39 x 22"
(99 x 55.8 cm)
Philadelphia Museum of
Art. Given by Dr. A.S.W.
and Philip H. Rosenbach.
49-41-2
Catalogue no. 111 b

During the eighteenth century, men rivaled women in the splendor and elaborateness of their costumes. Although the breeches and coat of an outfit were often made of the same more serviceable material, the vest (or waistcoat) was usually of a finer fabric, handsomely embroidered or brocaded. Coats were cut so that the vest was always generously revealed, since it was by far the most elegant part of a gentleman's attire, and vests were displayed with great pride, as is evident in paintings from the period. More often than not, the vest was fully embellished with needlework, whereas the breeches and coat were embroidered merely along their edges. Philadelphia's wealthy and fashionable residents followed the styles of England and France, often importing their garments sight unseen; understandably, these were frequently ill fitting and required alteration by an experienced local tailor.

Partly made garments also were imported from France. Shipped in the form of flat patterns set out on lengths of silk fabric, these were already embroidered with elaborate designs for coats, breeches, and vests. The patterns were then individually fitted, cut, and sewn together.

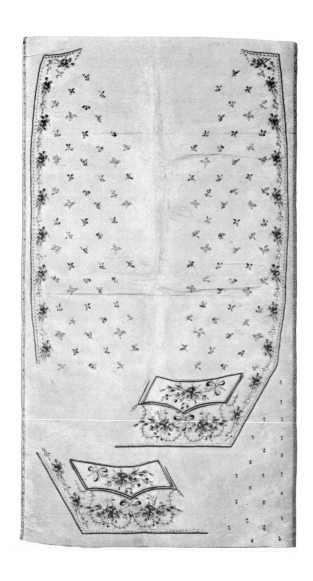

John Hesselius
(1728–1778)
Lynford Lardner
1749
Oil on canvas, 39¼ x 32"
(99.7 x 81.3 cm)
Private Collection
Catalogue no. 37

In 1749, according to his account book, Lynford Lardner, Keeper of the Great Seal of Pennsylvania, paid £6 to John Hesselius for "drawing my picture." This portrait of Lardner is the first known work by John Hesselius, the son of the Swedish-born painter Gustavus Hesselius, done when the artist was only twenty-one. Very often, Colonial painters based their poses on those found in British engravings, sometimes copying them outright but more often simply using them as a point of departure. Generally, then, the sitter had to pose only for the head and hands, since the posture and elegant gestures had already been borrowed from the printed model. This common practice sometimes resulted in such anatomical inconsistencies as Lardner's awkward right hand, which is not properly balanced on his hip.

John Hill (1770-1850)
after Joshua Shaw
(1777-1860)
View near the Falls of Schuylkill
From *Picturesque Views of American Scenery*
1820-21
Etching and aquatint with watercolor, 20⅞ x 14″ (53 x 35.6 cm)
The Library Company of Philadelphia
Catalogue no. 208

Tucker and Hemphill
China Factory (1826–38)
Vase
About 1832–35
Decorated by Thomas
Tucker
Porcelain, height 14¼"
(36.1 cm)
Philadelphia Museum of
Art. Given by Eliza
Amanda Tucker in
memory of Thomas
Tucker. 31-55-1
Catalogue no. 249

"In no quarter of the globe are the majesty and loveliness of nature more strikingly conspicuous than in America. The vast regions which are comprised in or subjected to the republic present to the eye every variety of the beautiful and sublime." This introduction to Joshua Shaw's *Picturesque Views of American Scenery*, which was to become the cornerstone of published American landscape views, went on to lament the lack of topographical art, commenting that "America only, of all the countries of civilized man, is unsung and undescribed." Shaw's drawings made to fill this void concentrated on the scenery along the Eastern seaboard. Each view was accompanied by a description of the special virtues or historical significance of the site, and their author frequently waxed lyrical in describing the local light, flora, and fauna.

The text that faces this rustic view taken near the Falls of Schuylkill, calls it "romantic and picturesque" and extols the inspirational values of the landscape. The atmosphere is pervaded by the rosy light of sunset as a traveler leads his horse homeward down a rock-strewn path. The superb, evocative coloring is a tribute to the armies of nameless colorists to whom eighteenth- and nineteenth-century printmakers sent their works for enrichment before the advent of chromolithography.

The rustic scene painted on this vase—made by Thomas Tucker (1812–1890) as a family curiosity—is a view of America's first large-scale porcelain factory, which was founded by William Ellis Tucker in 1826. The factory was housed in the former city waterworks buildings on Chestnut Street at the Schuylkill River. On the right of the scene, smoke bellows from the bottle kiln in which the factory's porcelain was fired.

The amphora shape and the gilded bands and handles of this vase are characteristic English and French Empire-style forms that were copied throughout the factory's twelve-year history. A distinctive Tucker eccentricity, the small ceramic braces placed between the molded figures and the body of the vase kept the figured handles from sagging during firing. Bases of many Tucker urns and vases turn slightly upward at the corners, the result of excessive shrinkage during the initial bisque firing.

Dress
1740-50
Taffeta, linen underdress
with lace; center back
length 60" (152.4 cm)
Philadelphia Museum of
Art. Given by Mrs.
Rodolphe Meyer de
Schauensee and Mrs.
James M. R. Sinkler in
memory of Mrs. Lewis
Audenreid. 50-28-3 a, b
Catalogue no. 34

For most of the eighteenth century, dress styles remained fairly constant—wide skirts supported by panniers, split overskirts, three-quarter-length sleeves, and low décolletages (although the size and shape of panniers, fit of bodice, neckline, and trimming varied greatly). This dress of dark-green taffeta has a boned bodice ending in tabs. Very tight-fitting, it is laced in front in a manner typical of the first half of the century; a stiff, richly ornamented stomacher, or busk, might have been worn under the lacing. The extremely low, rounded neckline reveals the linen underdress, edged in lace ruffles at the neckline and at the ends of the sleeves. The skirt, trimmed with pinked ruching along its front edges, is opened wide to expose a full matching underskirt with two tiers of pleats and ruching above the hem.

Benjamin West
(1738-1820)
Jane Galloway
Probably 1759
Oil on canvas, 49¾ x
39¼" (126.4 x 99.7 cm)
Historical Society of
Pennsylvania,
Philadelphia
Catalogue no. 56

Benjamin West, born in Springfield, Pennsylvania, was the first native American painter to achieve an international reputation. His early study was mostly derived from books, and his ideas on art must have been largely formed by contemporary portraits, engravings, and the few European paintings available to him in America. West left Philadelphia in 1759, and after spending three years in Italy, settled in London, where he was received with such enthusiasm that he remained there the rest of his life, becoming a charter member of the Royal Academy, historical painter to the king, and president of the Royal Academy.

This portrait of a stylishly dressed young lady with a floral garland is probably one of the last works that West painted before leaving for Europe. Jane Galloway (1745-1801), the daughter of wealthy Maryland Quakers, was orphaned at age three. According to her mother's will, "Jenny" was to be the ward of her oldest stepbrother, Samuel Galloway, who in 1756 began the construction of Tulip Hill, one of the finest surviving Georgian mansions in Maryland. While Tulip Hill was being built, Jenny spent much of her time visiting relatives in Philadelphia, and it was here that West painted her portrait. An entry in Samuel Galloway's account book for July 6, 1759, lists Jenny's purchase of a "blue satin Hatt," in all likelihood the one that appears in this portrait.

Richard Humphreys
(1750–1832)
Presentation Urn
1774
Silver, height 21½"
(54.6 cm)
David Beckwith Taylor,
Jr., Leland, Mississippi
Catalogue no. 102

This imposing tea urn by Richard Humphreys is generally considered the first silver object of neoclassical design manufactured in the Colonies. Since it was made in 1774, when the Adam brothers in England were just developing this new style in architecture, the urn must have been based directly on an English example—perhaps one imported by Humphreys between the time he set up his shop in 1772 and the tea embargo in 1773. With the exception of the florid cartouche with its inscribed dedication, typical of fine Philadelphia midcentury engraving still in use in 1774, the stylistic features of this urn—its square base, fluted banding, and the squared profile of its handles—are about fifteen years ahead of their time in Philadelphia. There is little doubt that the urn was much admired and talked about when it was presented by the Continental Congress to its Secretary, Charles Thomson, in 1774. Despite the imminent Revolution, it is surprising that no other piece of early neoclassical silverwork is known to have been made in America.

High Chest
About 1775
Mahogany, height 96¾"
(245.7 cm)
Philadelphia Museum of
Art. Given by Mrs.
Henry V. Greenough.
57-129-1
Catalogue no. 104 a

Sturdy and of commanding scale, this high chest features carved decoration that is, in conception, more sophisticated than any other produced in America before the Revolution. Colonial carvers rarely exceeded the structural boundaries of their pieces, and although he had every opportunity to produce a more flamboyant design here, the carver's exuberance remains well under control. His fine craftsmanship is seen in the crisply organized foliage on the marvelously secure legs, the garlands of vines and flowers on the corner quarter columns, and the flower-decked urns and pierced screen on the pediment. But the focus of his work appears in the decoration of the lowest central drawer, carved with a motif from Aesop's fable "The Fox and the Grapes." The fox, with his bushy tail, is shown framed by an elegant C-scroll, looking up at the sweet ripe grapes—which, lest there be any mistake about the episode portrayed, are directly over his nose. The moral of the tale advises: " 'Tis matter of skill and address, when a man cannot honestly compass what he would be at, to appear easy and indifferent upon all repulses and disappointments."

Charles Willson Peale
(1741–1827)
Staircase Group
1795
Oil on canvas, 89⅝ x
39½" (227.6 x 100.3 cm)
Philadelphia Museum of
Art. Purchased: The
George W. Elkins
Collection. E 45-1-1
Catalogue no. 137

Charles Willson Peale assumed a leading role in the attempt to establish an art academy in Philadelphia, the Columbianum, in 1794, and he was instrumental in the founding of the Pennsylvania Academy of the Fine Arts in 1805. The *Staircase Group* was painted as a showpiece for the first and only exhibition of the Columbianum, in May 1795, in the Senate Chamber of the State House (Independence Hall). One of the most famous of American paintings, this "deception" was clearly painted to deceive the viewer with its confusing intermingling of art and reality, and thus to impress the public with the artist's extraordinary ability.

The *Staircase Group* shows two of the artist's sons, Titian and Raphaelle, in life size, ascending a winding stairway typical of Philadelphia's simple domestic architecture. Raphaelle, in the foreground, holds a palette and maulstick; Titian peers out from the frame, a few steps higher. Before painting the picture, the elder Peale apparently had an actual staircase constructed on which to pose his sons. The finished painting was inserted into a doorframe and a real step was added at the base to expand the illusion. With these devices, Peale made it appear as if his sons were climbing a real staircase behind a doorway leading into the Columbianum exhibition gallery. Later, the painting was moved to Peale's Museum, where the deception was so successful that, according to the artist's son Rembrandt, George Washington once mistook these convincingly painted figures for living ones and bowed to them politely as he passed.

Gilbert Stuart
(1755–1828)
Mrs. Thomas Lea
About 1798
Oil on canvas, 29 x 24"
(73.6 x 60.9 cm)
Private Collection
Catalogue no. 147

The freshness of color, loose drawing, and lush application of paint in Gilbert Stuart's *Mrs. Thomas Lea* is in total contrast to the carefully detailed naturalism of the Peale tradition. Stuart's sensuous indulgence in the rich texture of the brushstroke is alien to Charles Willson Peale's highly finished flat surface and controlled linear style. Stuart's European training had led him to place less emphasis on likeness alone and more on aesthetic consideration of the portrait as an effective picture.

Stuart's much-sought portraits were undoubtedly considered more "stylish" than Peale's since they more closely reflected then-current English models. As the eccentric, temperamental "genius" who arrived in Philadelphia with an established European reputation, Stuart furnished a sharp contrast to Peale's "anyone can paint if trained" attitude. Women, especially, liked Stuart's more idealized portraits. In 1804, while she was standing in the elder Peale's studio in the presence of both Peale and his son Rembrandt, one woman begged the engaging Stuart to begin her portrait—obviously to the embarrassment of the Peales. Charles Willson Peale and Stuart became unquestionable rivals, and Stuart's greater success may have entered into Peale's decision, about 1796, to give up painting and concentrate on his art gallery and natural history museum.

Edward A. Goodes
(1832–1910)
Fishbowl Fantasy
1867
Oil on canvas, 30 x 25⅛"
(76.2 x 63.8 cm)
Private Collection
Catalogue no. 329

Although the Philadelphia sign painter Edward Goodes is known to have completed other paintings, his reputation as an artist rests solely on the fame of this disquieting still life. The bowl with its lavish array of flowers, instead of showing stems immersed in water through its clear glass, improbably contains three plump goldfish. The surface reflection gives a glimpse of two well-dressed women walking along a city street. The accessories of a woman's costume—a hat, some lace, a fan, a cross on a chain—appear to have been casually discarded on the table; the gloves, still retaining the shape of the hands that wore them, a calling card with the name "Isabel," and the folded letter suggest that these are the belongings of a specific woman.

How far Goodes intended this still life to be a symbolic portrait of a woman is impossible to tell. But the harsh colors and brittle linearity of the forms, the disconcerting stare of the goldfish, and the intrusion of the street scene prevent any passive contemplation of this composition. Instead of appealing to the senses with the placid sensuality expected of a typical Victorian still life, the tensions of form and color in this crowded mingling of flowers and objects stir the mind and invite the kinds of speculation about its meaning not usually associated with the work of an American artist in the nineteenth century.

Dressing Gown
1854
Wool, lined in silk;
center back length 57"
(144.7 cm)
Philadelphia Museum of
Art. Given by Agnes
Davisson Loughran.
58-6-4 a,b
Catalogue no. 299

Wedding Dress
1854
Silk taffeta, waist 26"
(66 cm)
Philadelphia Museum of
Art. Given by Agnes
Davisson Loughran.
58-6-1
Catalogue no. 298

When Catherine Heron of Philadelphia wore this
lavishly detailed pink dress to her wedding in 1854,
she was following the height of fashion. The
abundant silhouette of the three profuse, fully
gathered flounces, worn over a stiff crinoline or
hoop undergarment, is echoed by the capelet and
bell-shaped sleeves. The brilliant red dressing gown,
ornamented with braid in an Oriental design, was
also part of Catherine Heron's trousseau. It was
meant to be worn at home over all the usual
undergarments except the hoop. The fashion for
dressing gowns did not escape the censure of
Victorian moralists who equated the wearing of
these less-confining garments with the loosening of
manners and morals.

Charles Sheeler
(1883–1965)
Staircase, Doylestown
1925
Oil on canvas, 25⅛ x
21⅛" (63.8 x 53.7 cm)
Hirshhorn Museum and
Sculpture Garden,
Smithsonian Institution,
Washington, D.C.
Catalogue no. 449

This painting of a pre-Revolutionary house near Doylestown, Pennsylvania, which Charles Sheeler and his colleague Morton Schamberg rented for summer weekends of sketching and painting, is one of the finest expressions of Sheeler's persistent search for order and structure in the visual world. The lucid organization of a detail of eighteenth-century architecture here becomes one with the painter's structuring of his composition. Though concentrating on a real and specific subject, Sheeler achieves a pronounced degree of abstraction. Unessential detail is eliminated, and the painter's viewpoint is fixed with great precision and selected with an attention to the "framing" edge borrowed from his own extensive use of the camera. In 1938, Sheeler stressed the impact of his Doylestown years: "Interest in early American architecture and crafts has, I believe, been as influential in directing the course of my work as anything in the field of painting. The way in which a building or a table is put together is as interesting to me, and as applicable to my work, as the way in which a painting is realized."

Wharton Esherick
(1887-1970)
Desk and Bench
1931
Black walnut, ebony, and
padouk wood with
leather seat; desk height
49" (124.4 cm)
York K. Fischer,
West Cornwall,
Connecticut
Catalogue no. 458

In 1940, the architect George Howe analyzed the unique style and superb craftsmanship of Wharton Esherick's furniture: "The peculiar quality of the sculptor's products comes from the fact that he actually lives and works on a Pennsylvania hillside among the trees—oak, hickory, walnut and cherry—which he cuts down, seasons in his lumber yard, and tools with his own hands. Every form is a result of his personal sense of the direction of the grain and natural color value of the wood, and every surface is determined by his feeling for the infinite variety of the sense of touch."

This unusual desk made a decade earlier represents Esherick's cubist style, which emerged during the 1930s. The strongly sculptural form is a studied composition of triangular and trapezoidal shapes, and the hinged top and the writing compartment as well as the bench are all absorbed into the total design conception.

Oskar Stonorov
(1905-1970)
*Carl Mackley Houses
(Juniata Park Project)*
Castor Avenue and M
Street, between Cayuga
and Bristol streets
1932-34

Represented by:
*Carl Mackley Houses:
Isometric Rendering*
About 1933
From Carl Mackley
Houses brochure
Offset lithograph,
5⁹/₁₆ x 5⅞" (14.1 x
14.9 cm)
Private Collection
Catalogue no. 462

The Carl Mackley Houses embody the youthful idealism and social architecture of Oskar Stonorov, whose apparent aim was the reconstruction of the entire urban environment. In 1932, when he was twenty-seven years old, Stonorov moved to Philadelphia expressly to undertake the design of the Carl Mackley Houses for a small labor union, the Federation of Full Fashioned Hosiery Workers. The first housing project financed by the federal government under the New Deal, it brought to the United States advanced ideas of social architecture, and established Stonorov as a leading housing designer.

The project, occupying a full city block, comprises four parallel rows of three-story apartment buildings. The masonry facades are broken by projecting bays and recessed balconies (called "porches" in deference to the local row-house practice). The projecting wings at the ends of each building block create intimate spaces, suggestive of landscaped courtyards. The entire project, free of roadways, is unified by a network of walkways passing under the buildings and interconnecting extensive paved outdoor areas.

This statement of collective living embraces generous dwelling spaces, privacy, and landscaped amenity; but more remarkable for 1932, it includes swimming and wading pools, rooftop nursery schools and mechanical laundries, community kitchens, dining rooms, and meeting rooms—and a garage for every car. These anticipations of future higher standards of living have contributed to the survival of the Carl Mackley Houses, now nearly half a century old.

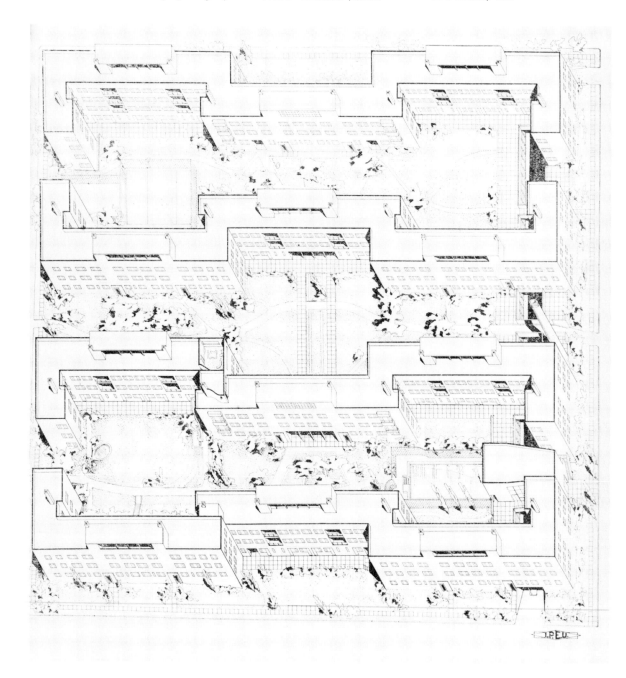

Benton Murdock
Spruance
(1904-1967)
Repose in Egypt
1940
Lithograph, 15⅜ x 10⅛"
(39 x 25.7 cm)
Philadelphia Museum
of Art. Purchased: Lola
Downin Peck Fund from
the Carl and Laura
Zigrosser Collection.
73-12-148
Catalogue no. 473

Throughout his career, Benton Spruance expressed concern for social justice and equality in his works on moral and religious themes. The same simplified, richly modeled figures of this lithograph, a modern representation set among skyscrapers of the biblical journey of the Holy Family into Egypt, had previously appeared as the central family group in a mural called *The Strength of Democracy Abides with the Family*. Based on a sketch of a family waiting for a bus to take them on a day's outing, the group, although used in two different contexts, has been transformed into one basic, universal symbol of human dignity. Spruance, who wished his work to appeal to a wide audience, believed that the great tradition of western art "commands all creative men to work, integrated into the civilization in which they live, to use as their symbols the broadly understood symbols of the people, and to use them in such a way that their aesthetic value is communicable to all."

Charles C. Fahlen
(born 1939)
Untitled
1973
Wood, fiber glass, and
resin; height 67"
(170.1 cm)
Charles C. Fahlen,
Philadelphia
Catalogue no. 523

Charles Fahlen's sculptures convey a sense of mysterious purpose in their construction, a mixture of practicality and hidden, symbolic content endowing their abstract forms with elusive meaning. The imposing presence of this pyramid raised on three stout, roughly carved wooden legs suggests that it was made for some particular use (perhaps as a dwelling, perhaps as a monument), but ultimately it resists interpretation as anything but art.

Fahlen is preoccupied with the specific properties of the materials he uses, materials heretofore not readily associated with the making of art. Much of his attention focuses on the task of choosing his materials and then on the process of constructing his works. The irregular, wrinkled surface of this pyramid, made of three pieces of cast translucent polyester resin, yields a variety of effects depending on the intensity and direction of the light that falls on it. But the material properties of Fahlen's pyramid do not explain its mystery; somehow, the artist's "fantasy," which suggested the form of the sculpture, summons up a corresponding fantasy, memory, or association within each viewer.

Barkley L. Hendricks
(born 1945)
*Ralph and Alvin
(Sickkayou)*
1974
Oil and acrylic on
canvas, 72 x 60" (182.9 x
152.4 cm)
Mr. and Mrs. Leonard
Davis, New York
Catalogue no. 538

The word "Sickkayou," the subtitle of this painting, is a slang expression of high praise in the dance world, elicited by a particularly deft step or a beautifully executed movement, and it well suits the informal mood of this painting. Ralph and Alvin, two dancers, are lightly poised on the very edge of the canvas, gazing out at the viewer with amused but noncommittal stares. Barkley Hendricks handles his portraits with a compelling mixture of cool and affection, locking his subjects within formal compositions of austere precision. Often humorous, occasionally aggressive, always provoking an immediate and personal reaction from the viewer, his models invite our admiration for their stance and style, and arouse our curiosity as to their identity. Unlike many contemporary exponents of realism, whose treatment of the human figure emphasizes the structure of the body or focuses on the textures of skin or clothing, Hendricks retains the portrait painter's fundamental concentration on the personalities of his subjects.

Embroidered Picture
1711
Wool and silk on linen,
22 x 28" (55.9 x 71.1 cm)
Philadelphia Museum of
Art. Purchased: Thomas
Skelton Harrison Fund.
43-77-1
Catalogue no. 11

Embroidered pictures, which appear to have
developed as a distinct form of needlework in
England during the sixteenth and seventeenth
centuries, were brought to America soon afterward.
They employed a limited number of motifs,
including this common pastoral theme of a
fashionably attired shepherd and shepherdess
reposing in a highly ornamental, idyllic setting.
Influenced by English tapestries of the period, the
typical work reflected the Jacobean aversion to
empty space. With its more open arrangement,
however, this composition probably derives its form
from the kind of embroidery—today known as
crewelwork—in which floral sprigs and other
conventional devices were used to embellish
furnishings and clothing. This decorative aesthetic
was contemporary with the fashion for imported
India chintz.

Benjamin West
(1738-1820)
The Death of Socrates
About 1756
Oil on canvas, 34 x 41"
(86.4 x 104.1 cm)
Private Collection
Catalogue no. 52

Benjamin West's earliest history picture, *The Death of Socrates,* is his only signed American work. West was about eighteen when he painted the picture in Lancaster, Pennsylvania, where he was visiting friends in order to execute portrait commissions. There he met William Henry, a wealthy gunsmith, who urged him to paint historical subjects and commissioned this work, which he based partially on an engraving by French artist Hubert-François Gravelot. *The Death of Socrates,* in its expression of an heroic ideal, a moment when man's dignity approaches that of the gods, is intended to elevate and ennoble the viewer. History painting in the spirit of this work was to become the special domain of Benjamin West, and no other English or American painter of his time equaled West's fame in this genre.

Jacob Eichholtz
(1776–1842)
*An Incident of the
Revolution*
1831
Oil on canvas, 48½ x 66"
(123.2 x 167.6 cm)
Museum of Fine Arts,
Boston. M. and M.
Karolik Collection
Catalogue no. 243

Although *An Incident of the Revolution* illustrates an actual event from history and points out a moral lesson, the choice of this subject—an amusing, minor incident—indicates a conception of the kind of event appropriate for an historical composition that is entirely different from artistic tradition. The episode, reported in Green's *Anecdotes of the War*, concerns the famous Revolutionary general Charles Lee, who had a reputation for negligence in dress and eccentricity in manners. Riding in advance of Washington and his troops one day, Lee is mistaken for a servant by a kitchen maid, who puts him to work in return for a cold meal. The artist shows the climactic moment when Washington arrives and the embarrassed girl realizes her mistake. Unabashed, Lee turns to an aide-de-camp with the moral of the story: "You see, young man, the importance of wearing your coat whole at the elbows, when, if even a general neglects it, a country girl can turn him to a scullion."

This first attempt at history painting by Jacob Eichholtz, a primarily self-taught portrait painter from Lancaster, Pennsylvania, suggests that the artist was conscious of the academic precedent that established the representation of historical subjects as a more elevated pursuit than portraiture. The broad landscape, the idealized portrait of George Washington, and the other figures carefully posed to emphasize the story reflect his understanding of the tradition of history painting, which he admired but did not usually practice.

Rembrandt Peale
(1778-1860)
The Roman Daughter
1811
Oil on canvas, 84½ x
62¼" (214.6 x 158.1 cm)
Webster, Inc., Fine Art,
Chevy Chase, Maryland
Catalogue no. 178

The Roman Daughter is based on an ancient legend of remarkable filial devotion. The story tells of an elderly Roman political prisoner, Cimon, who is condemned to starve to death, and his courageous daughter, Pero, who secretly sustains him during prison visits with milk from her own breast. When this scheme is discovered, Cimon receives a full pardon and is released. Rembrandt Peale considered this story of heroic loyalty and sacrifice, with its emphasis on the virtuous character of Pero, a fitting subject for his first attempt at history painting. Peale, Charles Willson Peale's second son, began painting oil portraits at the age of thirteen. The grandiose, historical compositions that he saw in Parisian studios during his visits to France in 1808 and 1809-10 apparently raised his ambitions beyond standard portraiture for upon his return to Philadelphia he painted a large equestrian portrait of Napoleon, which he displayed in 1811 in his newly opened picture gallery. Peale's calculated attempt to make a grander name for himself collapsed a year later when *The Roman Daughter* was shown at the Pennsylvania Academy and was criticized as unoriginal and unsuitable for public exhibition.

Thomas Eakins
(1844–1916)
William Rush Carving
His Allegorical Figure of
the Schuylkill River
1877
Oil on canvas, 20⅛ x
26⅛" (51.1 x 66.3 cm)
Philadelphia Museum of
Art. Thomas Eakins
Collection. 29-184-27
Catalogue no. 350

Instead of choosing an event from history or literature for the subject of this history painting, Thomas Eakins depicted a scene from the life of Philadelphia's first important sculptor William Rush, whose work he greatly admired. Rush is shown in his studio, carving the statue of a water nymph holding a bittern that he made in 1809 for the waterworks in Centre Square. To simulate an authentic pose, the young model holds a heavy book as a substitute for the weight of the bird. The sculptures ranged around the walls of Rush's shop are known to have been made at different times in his career, and thus the painting is not so much confined to a single moment in time, but rather seems to summarize Rush's continuing efforts as an artist. This, as well as the fact that the sculptor is carving a draped figure from the pose of a nude model, has led to the interpretation of this painting

as Eakins's justification of his own insistence on study directly from the nude, at a time when the use of nude models in life classes was a controversial issue at the newly reopened Pennsylvania Academy of the Fine Arts. When this painting was exhibited in New York in 1878 the critic for the *Times* was disturbed by "the presence in the foreground of the clothes of the young woman, cast carelessly over the chair. This gives a shock which makes one think about nudity—and at once the picture becomes improper."

Sidney Goodman (born 1936)
Room 318
1971-72
Oil on canvas, 75 x 97"
(190.5 x 246.3 cm)
Whitney Museum of American Art, New York. Purchased with the aid of funds from the National Endowment for the Arts (and exchange)
Catalogue no. 517

How remote this ordered composition appears from Eakins's study of a nude in a sculptor's studio! Yet it too forms part of the continuing tradition of figural painting in Philadelphia. Eakins's painting is all clutter and activity: the sculptor carves, the chaperone knits, the model's discarded clothes are strewn on a chair in the foreground. Goodman's austere studio is devoid of action, and the artist's participation is itself scarcely implied. In both paintings it is the arresting presence of the nude model, accented and bathed in light, that forms the visual and emotional center. Although based on careful observation of his subject, Sidney Goodman's paintings are rarely straightforward records of a particular place or scene. Working with individual elements that are each thoroughly scrutinized, he fits together a composition out of the separate parts, unifying them with a cool, silvery light.

Howard Roberts
(1843–1900)
La Première Pose
1873-76
Marble, height 51¼"
(130.1 cm)
Philadelphia Museum of
Art. Given by Mrs.
Howard Roberts.
29-134-1
Catalogue no. 338

Howard Roberts, like many of his colleagues at the Pennsylvania Academy of the Fine Arts in the 1860s, left for Paris to continue his artistic training at the Ecole des Beaux-Arts. Returning to Philadelphia in 1869, he set up a studio on Chestnut Street, but traveled again to Paris in 1873. During the next three years there, he completed this marble, *La Première Pose* ("The First Pose"), which he brought back to Philadelphia in time for exhibition at the Centennial exposition, where it earned one of three medals given to American sculpture. The contemporary critic William J. Clark, Jr., lavished praise on this work: "In the United States Department there was no piece of sculpture which was marked by such high technical qualities as the *Première Pose* of Howard Roberts—a work which was almost as much a product of the schools of Paris as the admirable performances exhibited in the French Department."

Indeed, Roberts's years in Paris had taught him to create a work that was very much within the tradition of French academic sculpture. Its pose—one seen daily in the life classes at the Ecole—and its subject—a model posing for a life study—were standard academic practice. However, Roberts adds pathos to the subject through the shielding posture of the left arm and the downcast eyes, suggesting that this is the young woman's first experience as a studio model, a situation wryly commented on by the little heads of Tragedy and Comedy at the top of the chair. The nude is rendered with a sensuousness and knowledge that completely reveal the artist's long and rigorous academic training in Paris with its great emphasis on drawing from the model and study of anatomy. This same power of observation is carried to all other aspects of the work, and the variety and detail of the surfaces, right down to the graining in the planks of the platform, are rendered with an almost obsessive attention to literal fact.

Thomas Eakins
(1844–1916)
Nude Woman, Seated,
Wearing a Mask
1865–66
Charcoal on paper, 24¼
x 18⅝" (61.6 x 47.3 cm)
Philadelphia Museum of
Art. Thomas Eakins
Collection. 29-184-49
Catalogue no. 328

The large number of oil sketches, perspective drawings, finished paintings, photographs, and sculpture that are recognized as Eakins's work provide an exceptional record of the range of his interests and of the development of his powers as an artist. But his student days at the Pennsylvania Academy of the Fine Arts and the Ecole des Beaux-Arts in Paris remain obscure. Relatively few of his drawings and paintings are known from the time when he was learning to be an artist through the repetitive drawing and painting exercises—first from casts of antique sculpture, then from nude models in life classes—which were the basis of the academic curriculum in his day.

This drawing exemplifies the kind of figure study very likely required of Eakins in life classes at the Pennsylvania Academy in 1865 or early in his Paris stay, before March 1867, when he began to paint his nude studies instead of drawing them in charcoal. Because the model is masked to conceal her identity (a standard practice in life classes at the Academy in Philadelphia until at least 1878), it has been assumed this drawing was made before Eakins left for Europe in the fall of 1866. If so, it shows a precocious talent and indicates that he not only already had an interest in what he later called the "grand construction" of the figure but had also developed an individual drawing style even before he went to Paris.

Charles Sheeler
(1883-1965)
Nude
1920
Conté crayon on paper,
4 x 5⅛" (10.2 x 13 cm)
Private Collection
Catalogue no. 444

The human figure was a rare subject for Charles Sheeler despite his years of training at the Pennsylvania Academy of the Fine Arts. But it is typical of Sheeler's deliberate, thoughtful method of working that, having decided to draw a nude figure, it should take on the impersonal monumentality of a sloping hillside. Most probably, Sheeler's approach to this drawing was suggested by his experience with the camera—if it was not indeed based on an actual photograph—and the technique of focusing on one area of the subject and cropping off the remainder was one that he had frequently employed in his photographic work. The soft, curving volumes of the woman's body become abstract elements as the human form dissolves into a serene and rhythmic composition, sensuous but devoid of emotion.

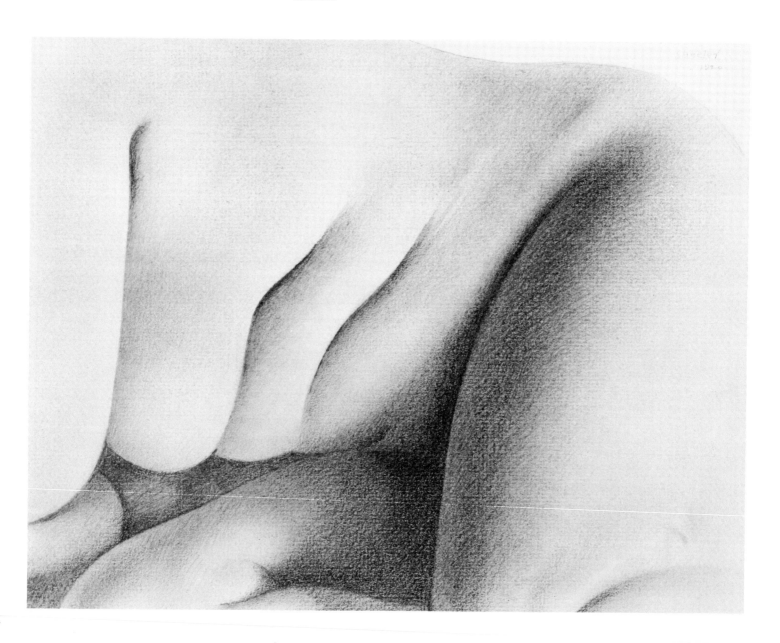

Arthur B. Carles
(1882-1952)
Abstraction (Last Painting)
1936-41
Oil on wood with cut paper and canvas, 40⅜ x 57½" (102.6 x 146 cm)
Hirshhorn Museum and Sculpture Garden, Smithsonian Institution, Washington, D.C.
Catalogue no. 478

The late works of Arthur B. Carles, who studied and taught at the Pennsylvania Academy of the Fine Arts, hold a unique position in the history of abstract art in America. *Last Painting* was an extraordinary achievement for the year 1941—let alone 1936, when it was probably begun. All trace of recognizable subject matter is gone, although a preliminary oil study for this painting was entitled *Nude*. Carles's eloquent color and his dynamic, sometimes dripping brushstrokes transform this painting into an important precursor of Abstract Expressionism. Not until the work of Willem de Kooning and Jackson Pollock was paint to be handled again with such authoritative violence.

Last Painting was probably still unfinished when a stroke forced Carles to abandon his work in December 1941. Nevertheless it powerfully conveys all his vigor and originality and prophesies a significant new movement in American art. What makes it particularly exciting is its full and exuberant palette, so characteristic of Carles's work throughout his life. As he reminded an interviewer in 1928: "If there's one thing in all the world I believe, it's *painting with color*. So damn few people paint with color, and what on earth else is painting for?"

John Sloan (1871–1951)
Anshutz on Anatomy
1912
Etching, 7⁵/₁₆ x 8⅞" (18.5
x 22.5 cm)
Philadelphia Museum of
Art. Purchased: Lessing J.
Rosenwald Gift and
Farrell Fund Income.
56-35-83
Catalogue no. 420

Thomas Eakins
(1844–1916)
The Gross Clinic
1875
Oil on canvas, 96 x 78½"
(243.8 x 199.3 cm)
Jefferson Medical
College, Thomas
Jefferson University,
Philadelphia
Catalogue no. 342

In 1875, at age seventy, Dr. Samuel David Gross
was widely known as a distinguished surgeon and
teacher. It is likely that Thomas Eakins witnessed
some of his lectures and demonstrations in anatomy
and surgery at Jefferson Medical College—as he
shows himself an attentive observer, sketching at
the right side of the painting. To heighten the drama
of this complex scene, Eakins emphasized the
poignant contrast between the cringing figure of a
woman—a relative of the patient, required by law to
be present at all charity operations—and the
impassive clerk recording the progress of the
surgical procedure.

When *The Gross Clinic* was exhibited in New York
in 1879, the critics, while finding the picture a work
of undeniable power, were nearly unanimous in
their rejection of the subject as unfit matter for art.
The critic for the *New York Tribune,* for example,
lashed out against it: "Here we have a horrible
story—horrible to the layman at least—told in all its
details for the mere sake of telling it and telling it
to those who have no need of hearing it. No purpose
is gained by this morbid exhibition, no lesson
taught—the painter shows his skill and the
spectator's gorge rises at it—that is all."

When Eakins was dismissed from the Pennsylvania
Academy of the Fine Arts for his dogmatic
insistence on study from the nude, Thomas
Anshutz, in a less dogmatic fashion, maintained the
Eakins tradition of intense anatomical study.
Although Anshutz is most frequently associated
with the Academy, where he taught for more than
thirty years, the anatomy lecture depicted in John
Sloan's *Anshutz on Anatomy* is one of a series held
for Robert Henri's class at the New York School of
Art. Much as Eakins did, Sloan has portrayed
himself in this scene as the figure with glasses in
the upper right, along with several other artists,
including Henri, William Glackens, and Maurice
Prendergast.

Frank Furness
(1839–1912) and
George Watson Hewitt
(1841–1916)
Pennsylvania Academy of the Fine Arts
Broad and Cherry streets
1871–76
Brick, limestone, sandstone, and brownstone construction, steel and cast-iron, granite columns, enamel plaques
Catalogue no. 335

Represented by:
Frederick Gutekunst
(1832–1917)
Pennsylvania Academy of the Fine Arts, Exterior from Northeast
About 1877
Photograph
Courtesy Pennsylvania Academy of the Fine Arts, Philadelphia

Designed in 1871 and finished in time for the Centennial in 1876, the Pennsylvania Academy of the Fine Arts is one of the most memorable structures in Philadelphia. The design by Frank Furness and George W. Hewitt reflects not only the vitality of the late nineteenth century but also their own distinct and vigorous personalities and training. Furness and Hewitt fused elements and principles from Gothic and classical architecture in an original alloy, which acknowledged the classical style as well as the modern English and French schools of architecture. French—and classic too—is the mansarded Broad Street facade, while the grooved triglyph blocks and sculpted panels stacked one above the other recall then popular French academic abstractions of classic design. The Gothic pointed arches, the floral ornamentation, and the strident architectural polychromy—red brick, yellow-tan

limestone, purple-ish-brown brownstone, brilliantly toned enamel plaques, and pink granite columns—are carryovers from the English school, and John Ruskin's fervent praise of the Venetian Gothic style. Thus it is a highly eclectic facade, but with a point, for it demonstrates in the art academy building the oneness of architecture.

The public galleries and the private teaching spaces are clearly differentiated on the exterior with the student entrance off the less traveled Cherry Street and the public entrance on Broad Street, leading into a brilliantly colored and skylighted stairwell crowned by a coved ceiling glittering with silver stars on a field of blue. Beyond, a succession of skylighted galleries, deep-toned in plum and ochre, displayed the famed Academy collection.

Willis G. Hale (about 1849–1907)
Peter A. B. Widener Mansion
Broad Street and Girard Avenue
1886
Catalogue no. 362

Represented by:
Exterior of Widener Mansion
Photograph
Courtesy Free Library of Philadelphia

Set prominently at the intersection of two of Philadelphia's principal streets, the Widener Mansion remains as an example of opulence in domestic architecture that is unmatched in Philadelphia. Its architect Willis G. Hale designed the mansion with an immense, symmetrical facade flanked with conically roofed towers. The facade curves around the corner towers and bows out around the bay on the side in a manner which seems to anticipate the sinuosity of the European Art Nouveau style of the next decade. The walls are embellished with vast quantities of ornamental detail, typical of most of Hale's projects. The rusticated stone basement is carved to simulate a woven surface of criss-crossing stone blocks, the upper walls are garlanded, and ordered with pilasters and belt courses, while here and there niches are carved with floral bouquets.

As remarkable as the exterior is, it is overshadowed by the principal spaces of the interior, where Hale's talents were enhanced by the skills of the Austrian-trained "decorative artist" George Herzog. In the stair hall, Herzog applied splendid materials to embellish all of the available surfaces. In the extraordinary wainscotted dining room with its musicians' gallery and gigantic fireplace, Herzog painted away the plaster walls providing imaginary views out of the room into sunny gardens and picturesque Northern Renaissance townscapes peopled by Widener's own children in plumed hats and cavalier dress. For a moment, in one confined space, the Victorian search for a present in the past found its reality. Time and space were transcended in the joint vision of Hale, Herzog, and their client Peter A. B. Widener.

John Hewson
(About 1745–1821)
Printed Coverlet
About 1780–1800
Cotton and linen, 102¾
x 105" (260.9 x 266.7 cm)
Philadelphia Museum of
Art. Given by Joseph B.
Hodgson, Jr. 30-100-1
Catalogue no. 123

John Hewson was one of the first calico printers recorded in Philadelphia, and his work helped to lay the foundation on which the city's great textile industry was built. With experience gained in London and a recommendation from Benjamin Franklin, Hewson and his family immigrated to Philadelphia late in 1773. The next summer he established his calico works at Kensington in the Northern Liberties, near the Aramingo Canal, which provided the clear water needed for the bleaching process. Although imported fabrics were generally more sophisticated, Hewson's locally made prints soon became popular in Philadelphia. This coverlet is a rare and handsome example of Hewson's work. The cloth was woven on a narrow loom in two widths, and then sewn together with a seam down the middle, as was typical of coverlets until about 1820. The delicate block-printed design of a vase of

flowers, surrounded by flowery sprigs, birds, and butterflies, has much in common with the patterns of chintz imported from India. Each of the three borders surrounding the center square is of a different design, and the corners are printed with separate blocks, a method typical of early printers.

Michel Bouvier
(1792–1874)
Card Table
About 1830
Maple and white pine,
height 30" (76.2 cm)
Mr. and Mrs. Donald L.
Fennimore, Wilmington,
Delaware
Catalogue no. 240

Born in France and trained there in cabinetry, Michel Bouvier immigrated to New York, where he soon became a successful carpenter. In 1817 he settled permanently in Philadelphia and established his own cabinetmaking shop. Among his first important patrons was his compatriot Joseph Bonaparte, Napoleon's brother and the ex-king of Spain, who lived in exile near Bordentown, New Jersey. Through his work for Bonaparte, Bouvier later came to the attention of Stephen Girard, a fellow emigré who had amassed a fortune in America, and other wealthy Philadelphians.

Among the great documented pieces of Philadelphia classical revival furniture, this card table has a stenciled label bearing the address (91 South Second Street) where Bouvier's cabinet and sofa warehouse was located between 1825 and 1844. The table is

based on forms found in English pattern books, but differs from foreign models in its handsome curly maple veneer, which was used frequently in Philadelphia. The white pine feet, ebonized for dramatic contrast with the golden maple and carved in the form of a claw under a curled leaf with scrolls behind, are also characteristic of Philadelphia cabinetry. *The Philadelphia Cabinet and Chair Makers Union Book of Prices* of 1828 described a table of this type as a "Pillar and Claw Card Table," listing it at $5.50.

Anthony G. Quervelle
(1789–1856)
Secretary Bookcase
1827
Mahogany, mahogany
veneer, and stained
burl ash; height 109½″
(278.1 cm)
Philadelphia Museum of
Art. Given by Mr. and
Mrs. Edward C. Page in
memory of Robert E.
Griffith. 60-159-1
Catalogue no. 229

An outstanding example of the arts of Philadelphia, this mahogany secretary bookcase is also one of the great masterpieces of American furniture. Its thorough documentation, which includes five labels ("Anthony G. Quervelle's Cabinet and Sofa Manufactory, 126 South Second Street a few doors below Dock, Philadelphia") and the fact that he chose to exhibit it at the Franklin Institute's 1827 exhibition of mechanical arts—where it was awarded a silver medal—surely indicate Quervelle's pride in the piece. According to the Franklin Institute's "Report of the Committee on Premiums and Exhibitions of the Fourth Annual Exhibition," of 1827, "they have carefully examined the different articles submitted to their inspection and are of opinion that the secretary and bookcase deposited by Mr. Anthony Quervelle is the best piece of furniture of that description exhibited for premium."

Here, as is often the case in American furniture, Quervelle borrowed certain motifs, as well as the overall composition, from several different European and American design sources. His main source appears to have been George Smith's *Cabinet-Maker and Upholsterer's Guide*, published in London in 1826. The same brilliantly figured mahogany veneers and circular insets, as well as the same overall architectonic organization, appear in both Smith's design and Quervelle's piece. The design of the muntins in the bookcase door is seen in the *Philadelphia Cabinet and Chair Makers Union Book of Prices* of 1828, while the gadrooning, flat carving, and the use of contrasting woods in the interior compartment and at the edge of the radiating fan are also to be found in Philadephia cabinetwork of the period.

Isaac Rehn
(active 1845-75)
*J. Elliot, John D. Huhn,
and Henry
Cowperthwait
Playing Chess*
1856
Ambrotype, 5½ x 4¼"
(14 x 10.7 cm)
The Franklin Institute,
Philadelphia
Catalogue no. 308

Isaac Rehn, a painter who in 1849 turned to photography, introduced the ambrotype process to Philadelphia in 1853. In this process, a glass negative, slightly underexposed and backed with a black substance, is able to give the effect of a positive image. The ambrotype was easier and less expensive than the daguerreotype, and permitted a shorter exposure time. Moreover, unlike the daguerreotype, the image was not necessarily reversed and there was no metallic glare to inhibit viewing it in any light. Ambrotypes are quite rare, for they were in vogue for only a short period, until about 1857, after which the tintype and paper print replaced them in popularity.

Although this ambrotype lacks the wide range of tones possible with the daguerreotype, it is an exquisite example of early photographic art. The treatment of the subject matter is somewhat exceptional. The depiction of three men playing chess is unusual, for most ambrotypes were straightforward portraits made as family mementos. Here, although the men are clearly portrayed, the pleasing qualities of the composition as a whole rather than the individual portraits of the chess players prevail.

71

Benjamin Randolph
(1721-1791) and Hercules
Courtenay (1744?-1784)
Easy Chair
1770-72
Mahogany, height 45¼″
(115 cm)
Philadelphia Museum of
Art. Purchased: Museum
Fund. 29-81-2
Catalogue no. 89

Benjamin Randolph, the cabinetmaker who made the famous lap desk on which Thomas Jefferson wrote the Declaration of Independence, has usually been given the credit for making this carved easy chair. It descended through his second wife's family, providing a solid provenance and, by association, attribution. However, since Randolph was trained as a joiner, not a carver, it is more reasonable to assume that the chair was produced in his cabinetmaking shop at the Sign of the Golden Eagle, on Chestnut Street, as a collaborative effort between joiner and carver, and then sent out to another craftsman for upholstery. Hercules Courtenay, Randolph's journeyman who arrived from London in 1765, probably executed the carving—the fine scrollwork, diaper patterning, and face motif on the apron and the handsome hairy paw feet. His carving reflects a thorough knowledge of English furniture design, which Courtenay would have learned both during his apprenticeship in London and from the design books he brought with him to America.

Charles Willson Peale
(1741-1827)
The John Cadwalader Family
1772
Oil on canvas, 51½ x 41¼" (130.8 x 104.8 cm)
Captain John Cadwalader, U.S.N.R. (Ret.), Blue Bell, Pennsylvania
Catalogue no. 92

Another piece of furniture from Benjamin Randolph's shop, one of a pair of card tables made for John Cadwalader (and still owned by his descendants), appears in this portrait of the Cadwalader family. The painting was commissioned in 1772 at the time the family was moving into their magnificent house on Second Street and furnishing it with the finest products of local craftsmanship. Cadwalader, a wealthy merchant, had signed the Non-Importation Agreement in 1765, and his steady patronage of Philadelphia's best craftsmen may have developed from a resolve to encourage American industry. Charles Willson Peale shows John Cadwalader with his wife and daughter in their new house proudly displaying what may have been their latest purchase, the card table on which little Anne is seated.

Edna Andrade (born 1917)
Cool Wave
1974
Acrylic on canvas, 72 x
72" (182.8 x 182.8 cm)
Luther W. Brady,
Philadelphia
Catalogue no. 537

Edna Andrade has expressed the aims of her art in a statement that links the sophisticated simplicity of a painting such as her *Cool Wave* with the venerable tradition of making patterns: "I find myself in the ancient tradition of all those anonymous artisans who have painted pottery and tiles, laid mosaic pavings, woven baskets and carpets, embroidered vestments and sewn quilts. Our tradition reaches back through eons of time to that genius who first drew a circle and used its magic." *Cool Wave* is one of a series of Andrade's paintings on the theme of a curve contained within a square. In each of twenty-five squares, radiating lines, meticulously drawn with a draftsman's ruling pen, meet an arc with radius equal to the length of one side of the square and with its centerpoint at one corner of the square. Arcs measured from the lower right corner of a square alternate with arcs measured from the upper left corner of the next to produce a regular, pulsating rhythm.

Needlework Pocketbooks
Left:
1774
Wool on linen canvas,
4⅛ x 5¹³/₁₆"(10.5 x
14.8 cm) (closed)
Right:
About 1755
Wool and silk on linen
canvas, 9⅛ x 6¹³/₁₆" (23 x
17.3 cm) (open)
Anne Chew Barringer,
Radnor, Pennsylvania
Catalogue no. 50

The effective blending of colors and shading of the jagged geometric shapes on these needlework pocketbooks are typical patterns associated with the Irish, or Florentine, stitch, with which they are worked. Pocketbooks such as these, made of worsted (crewel) yarns, were fashionable in America during the eighteenth century and achieved the height of their popularity between 1760 and 1780. The two most common forms are seen here. The one on the left consists of a pocket with a flap to fold over the opening like an envelope. The second pocketbook—inscribed with the name Samual Morgan—folds in the middle, with a pocket on each side. This type was generally, although not exclusively, used by men to carry papers and currency.

Miniatures were intended as symbols of a shared emotional bond—love, friendship, filial piety, or grief over the loss of a loved one. In an age when death and mourning were much more openly acknowledged than today, the mourning miniature was quite common. The traditional image for such miniatures included a classically garbed female weeping by a tomb, a funerary urn, and a weeping willow. Thomas Sully's 1801 memorial to his mother Sarah, in this form, must have been painted early in his professional painting career.

Anna Claypoole Peale, the fourth daughter of James Peale and niece of Charles Willson Peale, was an accomplished painter of miniatures. Anna's portrait of her cousin, Rubens Peale, wearing wire spectacles, is a charming and sensitively executed work, painted with a fine hatching technique in the face and figure, but treated more broadly in the background.

William Birch, best known for his engravings of Philadelphia scenes, always considered himself first an enamel painter, and his numerous pins, boxes, and miniatures received great acclaim. Birch's gold-bound enamel brooch depicts the Triumph of American Independence and proclaims America's victory in the War of 1812. Based on an engraving, it shows Liberty, or America, in Roman dress and crowned with a feathered headdress, riding in a chariot drawn by three prancing horses. Proudly she holds an American flag with fifteen stripes and stars, while beyond is a glimpse of the Capitol in Washington still under construction.

The silver whistle and bells, with its coral teething stick, a form that was often used, must have been treasured for it appears in a number of contemporary children's portraits. This example by John Leacock, goldsmith and jeweler at the Sign of the Golden Cup, on Front Street, elegantly incorporates the rather ungainly shaft into a successful design. The whistle end tapers comfortably and protrudes far enough so that the bells do not interfere with its use.

Gold, as popular as silver for small personal accessories during the Colonial period, was made into many of the forms that are still used today. Coats and vests featured engraved gold buttons, sleeves were held at the cuffs with gold links, shirts were fastened down the front with gold studs, and necklaces were clasped with gold fittings. The shoe buckle, however, is distinctly a relic of the eighteenth century, used to decorate men's soft kidskin shoes or silk pumps. Vulnerable even when reserved for special occasions, shoe buckles have scarcely survived, and this elaborate example, cast in gold, is rare if not unique. Despite its small scale, it exhibits the finely crafted ornamentation and superb design of Joseph Richardson, Sr., a member of the renowned family of Philadelphia silver- and goldsmiths.

Joseph Richardson, Sr.
(1711-1784)
Shoe Buckle
About 1740-50
Gold, length 1⅞"
(4.8 cm)
Yale University Art
Gallery, New Haven.
The Mabel Brady
Garvan Collection
Catalogue no. 35

Joseph Richardson, Jr.
(1752-1831)
Chatelaine Hook
1790-1800
Gold, length 2⁵/₁₆"
(5.8 cm)
Yale University Art
Gallery, New Haven.
The Mabel Brady
Garvan Collection
Catalogue no. 130

Edmund Milne
(1724-1822)
Locket (Clasp)
1764
Gold, length 1¹/₁₆"
(2.7 cm)
Yale University Art
Gallery, New Haven.
John Marshall Phillips
Collection
Catalogue no. 63

John Leacock (1729-1802)
Whistle and Bells
About 1756-58
Silver and coral, length
5¼" (13.3 cm)
Philadelphia Museum of
Art. Given by Mrs.
Thomas D. Thacher.
70-81-1
Catalogue no. 53

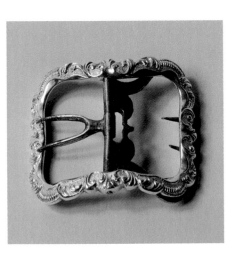

The goldsmith, Edmund Milne, a close associate of
Joseph Richardson, Sr., fashioned this necklace clasp
in 1764, decorating it with an engraved basket of
flowers. Frequently contrived in the form of a
hollow locket, like this example, clasps held the
strands of beads fastened to the small holes at each
side; most were fitted for three strands, but this,
which is fitted for four, is more unusual.

The chatelaine hook, used for carrying household
keys, was one of the simplest and most common
items made by eighteenth-century silversmiths.
However, gold examples such as this one by Joseph
Richardson, Jr., are quite rare. The shape of the hook
was determined by the need for a smooth fit over
the waistband of a skirt or apron; the back piece
was always longer than the front to balance the
weight of items suspended on chains. Each key was
attached with a chain long enough to reach the
keyhole of a door, desk, or box. Small scissors,
thimbles, pincushions, and needle cases were
sometimes also carried along with the keys.

Stanley Lechtzin (born 1936)
Torque (Necklace)
1972
Electroformed silver gilt and polyester, length 12⅛″ (30.8 cm)
Philadelphia Museum of Art. Given by the Friends of the Philadelphia Museum of Art. 73-94-7
Catalogue no. 518 b

The unusual and innovative forms of Stanley Lechtzin's jewelry are made possible by his experimentation with electroforming, a technique used for industrial purposes in the nineteenth century but adapted to the arts only in the past decade. In the electroforming process, an electrolytic deposit on a removable master form, or matrix, creates a hollow shell of metal, which can be relatively large yet light in weight. Here, Lechtzin has combined gilded electroformed silver with translucent plastic, another material originally produced for industrial purposes, to create a striking and original necklace. According to Lechtzin, who has lived in Philadelphia since 1962 and teaches at the Tyler School of Art, "I attempt to create personal values with materials and processes which today are used in a mechanical and anonymous manner by industry."

Attributed to John Maene
(1863–1928)
Vase
After 1902
Pottery with underglaze
decoration, height 8¼"
(21 cm)
Mr. and Mrs. Samuel
Ward, Moylan,
Pennsylvania
Catalogue no. 401

Some fifteen miles west of Philadelphia stands a cluster of houses and two old mill buildings called Rose Valley. The buildings' common architectural vocabulary of red-tile roofs, rough stone, and stucco inset with colored tile testify to their origin as largely the work of one man, the Philadelphia architect and Rose Valley resident William L. Price. The roots of Rose Valley lie in the last decade of the nineteenth century in William Morris's tract *News From Nowhere*, which describes an England of the not-too-distant future, with water again running clear, air no longer befouled by smoke, and people participating in every aspect of their lives.

In 1901, five years after Morris's death, such a community became reality at Rose Valley. The community was to be centered around creative work, and the mill buildings were adapted to the production of furniture, pottery, and other useful objects. Although the town corporation itself made nothing, it provided the work space and also acknowledged craftsmanship of high quality by conferring the town seal—a buckled belt (symbol of unity and brotherhood) encircling a wild rose with a letter "V" on its petals.

Potterymaking was one of the earliest activities of Rose Valley, and this double-handled vase is one of the few documented examples known to have survived. Unlike most other pottery produced at Rose Valley, John Maene's vase shows some influence of European Art Nouveau design, especially in the undulating curves of the handles and neck. The decoration is not stiffly applied to the form, but is subtly realized with drip glazes in a variety of soft, intermingling tones of green.

Samuel Yellin
(1885-1940)
Fire Screen
About 1925-30
Wrought iron, height 38″
(96.5 cm)
Harvey Z. Yellin—
Samuel Yellin
Collection, Philadelphia
Catalogue no. 455 a

Born in Galicia, Poland, in 1885, Samuel Yellin was apprenticed to a Russian blacksmith at age seven, becoming a master craftsman at seventeen. In accordance with local custom, he then set out to travel, spending three years in Belgium reproducing Gothic ironwork and armor. After two years in England he came to Philadelphia, where he set up a studio and organized ironwork classes at the Pennsylvania Museum and School of Industrial Art. His straightforward approach to ironwork is demonstrated in this fire screen, designed and executed for the massive fireplace at his studio on Arch Street. The intricate tendrils were formed by hammering thin iron strips while they were heated to cherry red and then fire welding them together. The entire decorative interior section was then attached to the frame by a series of small iron collars. Much of Yellin's work reveals a clear understanding of French Gothic design, and the naturalistic animal heads on each of the side supports hark back to earlier precedents. At the same time his work seems clearly rooted in the twentieth century. His understanding of the European Art Nouveau style can be seen in the repetitive rhythms of the wrought-iron tendrils.

Max Rosenthal
(1833–1919) after Collins
& Autenrieth (active
about 1854–1902)
*Grand Lodge Room of
the New Masonic Hall,
Chestnut Street,
Philadelphia*
Printed by Louis
Napoleon Rosenthal
1855
Chromolithograph, 21 x
26⅞" (53.5 x 68.2 cm)
The Library Company of
Philadelphia
Catalogue no. 302

Perhaps nowhere else in Philadelphia was the Gothic taste realized so magnificently as in the second Masonic Hall on Chestnut Street. Designed in 1853 by Samuel Sloan and John Stewart, the structure had lavishly appointed interiors presumably conceived by another Philadelphia firm, Collins & Autenrieth, who supplied the drawings for this impressive chromolithograph. The Grand Lodge Room on the second floor of the hall was ornamented and furnished in a highly coloristic ensemble of the Gothic-revival vocabulary. The designers arranged seats carved with Gothic motifs along the walls like choir stalls, in several rows leading to a central raised dais bearing an elaborately carved throne flanked by graceful statues in niches. The walls were ornamented with columns terminating in a delicate polychrome web of fan vaults interspersed with Masonic devices. The interior was calculated to have a breathtaking effect; dominant gold and blue hues evoked the richness and pageantry of a medieval throne room, as a suitable setting for the solemn Masonic rites. Louis N. Rosenthal took even more than his usual care in printing to achieve a harmonious tonality and perfect color registration. The chromolithograph glows, vibrant and jewel-like, long after the original has been destroyed.

George Howe
(1886–1955) and William
E. Lescaze (1896–1969)
*Philadelphia Saving
Fund Society*
Twelfth and Market
streets
1929–32
Brick, granite, limestone,
and marble sheathing
Catalogue no. 456

Represented by:
L. L. Malkus
*Philadelphia Saving
Fund Society*
1940
Pencil, 21¼ x 9¼" (53.9
x 23.5 cm)
Philadelphia Saving Fund
Society

Almost as soon as it was completed, the
Philadelphia Saving Fund Society (PSFS) building
had gained its reputation as one of the most
important American buildings of this century. This
streamlined tower was well received not only
because of the quality of its striking and ingenious
design, but also because it represented the most
direct application of the principles of European
modernism, the so-called International Style, to a
tall office building.

In addition to the absence of ornamentation and its
honest and direct use of materials, the building is
remarkable for the way its design expresses the
activities that occur within. The tall office shaft
surmounts a broader multistory base and is backed
by a service spine containing elevators, fire stairs,
and washrooms. Not content to differentiate these
various uses just by form and by changes in window
size, the architects sheathed each zone with a
different material—the service core with black
brick; the ground-floor shop and first-floor banking
room, with polished granite; and the office spire
with an envelope of brick spandrels and piers clad in
limestone and marble.

In designing the building, Howe and Lescaze also
assumed responsibility for the interior
appointments. Special attention was given to the
thirty-second floor executive area—the board room,
vestibules, and dining room. The low, heavily
padded "modern" armchair, part of a larger suite of
upholstered furniture, was designed for the vestibule
adjacent to the board room. Its comfortable stuffed
leather form subtly contrasts with the straight
wooden feet veneered in Macassar ebony. In the
main banking room and in many office spaces,
chrome-plated tubular-steel furniture was
introduced. This example, with leather upholstery,
is from the bank's safe deposit floor. Tubular metal
furniture, first manufactured in Europe in 1925,
began to be produced in this country in the late
1920s. Because of its potential for continuous lines,
this new medium achieved with ease what could
only be attained in wood with great difficulty—one
continuous member of arms, stiles, and supports.

Howe and Lescaze
Armchair
1932
Leather upholstery and
Macassar ebony veneer,
height 33″ (84 cm)
Philadelphia Saving Fund
Society
Catalogue no. 457 b

Howe and Lescaze
Armchair
1932
Chrome-plated tubular
steel, leather, height
32½″ (83 cm)
Philadelphia Saving Fund
Society
Catalogue no. 457 c

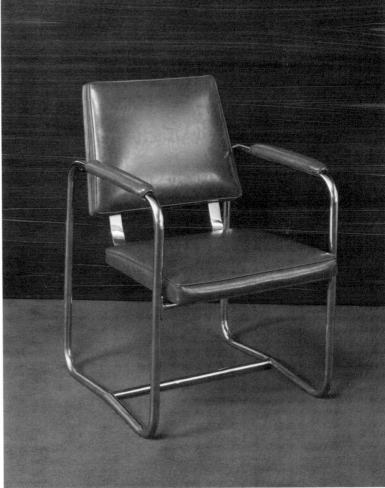

Charles Willson Peale
(1741–1827)
The Peale Family
1773 and 1808–9
Oil on canvas, 56½ x
89½" (143.5 x 227.3 cm)
The New-York Historical
Society
Catalogue no. 94

John Sartain (1808–1897)
after Christian Schussele
(1824?–1879)
*Men of Progress—
American Inventors*
1862
Mezzotint and etching,
21⅝ x 35⅝" (55 x 90.5
cm)
Historical Society of
Pennsylvania,
Philadelphia
Catalogue no. 319

This famous portrait of Charles Willson Peale's family was the first truly ambitious painting that Peale did after his return from London in 1769. Painted in 1773, it was evidently intended as a studio exhibition piece—an advertisement of Peale's great technical versatility. The occasion for the portrait is a drawing lesson. Turning from work on a painting of *The Three Graces*, Peale, palette and brushes in hand, supervises his brother St. George, who is making a sketch of their mother and one of Charles's daughters. The other family members grouped around the table are Peale's wife Rachel, another child, his brother James, his two sisters, and the family nurse, who stands at right.

In 1808, Peale wrote to his son Rembrandt that he was repainting the background of the group as well as his own head in order to achieve a better likeness. Because a mirror would have been useless for painting himself in this peculiar position, Peale improvised by working from the plaster self-portrait bust seen in the center of the mantel. With the addition of the head of the family dog, the work was finally completed in 1809 and placed not in the studio, but in Peale's Museum, where it must have added weight to the strong imprint of his personality on everything else in the collection.

Men of Progress is an imaginary grouping of some of the most inventive minds of the nineteenth century. Their skills ranged from medicine to mechanics, and all contributed to the growth of the United States as a nation and an industrial power. A portrait of Benjamin Franklin, father of all American inventors, presides over the assembly in the marble chamber, and a number of inventions and plans lie on the floor, as if discarded after a discussion.

At the far left, Dr. William Morton (1819–1868), discoverer of the anesthetizing effects of ether, stands close to James Bogardus (1800–1874), known for his development of cast-iron architecture. Samuel Colt (1814–1862), inventor of the repeating pistol, is shown next, with one of his patented revolvers below. Joseph Saxton (1799–1873), who established the United States standards of weights and measures, stands behind Cyrus McCormick (1804–1894), next to a model of his famous reaper.

In the group studying a telegraph are locomotive builder Peter Cooper (1791–1883), who leans over the shoulder of Charles Goodyear (1800–1860). At Goodyear's feet a galosh is upturned to show its vulcanized rubber sole. Also seated is Jordan Mott (1798–?), developer of a furnace that burned refuse coal; standing behind is Joseph Henry (1797–1878), pioneer of electromagnetic studies. Next come Eliphalet Nott (1773–1866) and Frederick Sickels (1819–1895), physicists who patented inventions dealing with heat and fuel conservation.

Samuel F. B. Morse (1791–1872), the former history painter and president of the National Academy of Design, and inventor of the telegraph, dominates the scene. He turns to Richard Hoe (1812–1886), inventor of the type-revolving printing press. Between them is Henry Burden (1791–1871), his horseshoe-making machine indicated by a model on the table in front of him. The standing figure is Erastus Bigelow (1814–1879), whose carpet loom appears in a plan on the wall behind.

The last three figures are Isaiah Jennings (1782–1862), inventor of threshing machines and instantaneous matches; Thomas Blanchard (1788–1864), best known for his turning lathes; and Elias Howe, Jr. (1819–1867), developer of the sewing machine. While not all of these names have become household words, Christian Schussele's painting, circulated by means of John Sartain's print, served as a visible reminder of a remarkable group of men who were the direct ancestors of Ford and Edison.

Benjamin Harbeson
(1728-1809)
Sundial
1763
Brass, diameter 5¾"
(14.6 cm)
Philadelphia Museum of
Art. Purchased: Joseph E.
Temple Fund. 20-99-1
Catalogue no. 61

John Vallance (about
1770-1823), Robert Scot
(active 1781-1820), and
others
*Encyclopaedia; or, a
Dictionary of Arts,
Sciences, and
Miscellaneous Literature*
1790-98
Published by Thomas
Dobson
Bound volume 10½ x
8⅛" (26.6 x 20.6 cm)
The Library Company of
Philadelphia
Catalogue no. 148

Sundials, used to set or to verify less reliable timepieces such as pocket watches, were made by silversmiths, clockmakers, scientific instrument makers, and in this instance, by a coppersmith, Benjamin Harbeson. Small sundials, made of silver or bone, were carried in the pocket; large ones, like this, were set out in gardens. Sundials generally are marked for standard daylight hours, but this one begins earlier, at five in the morning and extends to seven in the evening; hours are divided into eighths, with the longer lines marking the quarter hours and half hours.

Like many pre-Revolutionary craftsmen, Benjamin Harbeson carried civic responsibilities in addition to his shop and trade. He signed the Non-Importation Agreement of 1765, and was on the second Committee of Correspondence, in 1775, encouraging

home manufacture. The following year he became captain of the Second Battalion of Philadelphia Associates. After the war, Harbeson resumed his business at the Sign of the Golden Tea Kettle, on Market Street, and soon became the most prominent brass founder in Philadelphia.

From A to Zymosimeter, Thomas Dobson's eighteen-volume encyclopedia, copied after the third edition of the *Encyclopaedia Britannica* and published from 1790 to 1798, offered Americans the most comprehensive and attractive packaging of information then available on this continent. The illustrations, concise and numerous, reflect the best work of American artisan-engravers of that era. A work of this size and breadth was unprecedented in America, and Dobson had great difficulty rounding up the number of competent engravers required to produce the encyclopedia's 542 plates.

The elaborate frontispiece, furnished to the subscribers in 1798 after the eighteen volumes were completed, speaks dramatically for the whole publication, with its broad scope, variety of subjects, and grandeur of conception. Knowledge in all its branches is represented by a throng of philosophers, astronomers, mathematicians, artists, savants, alchemists, surveyors, craftsmen, heralds, and musicians—shown with all their accouterments in a classical architectural setting. An aerial balloon surveys the gathering, while in the distance Adam and Eve stand in a verdant landscape, surrounded by a group of animals. In a well-stocked library, figures in togas, hungry for knowledge, clamber among the books. Even for an engraver merely copying another frontispiece, this plate was very ambitious by American standards at that time. The delicate detail of the numerous instruments and diagrams and the intricacy of the allegorical and historical figures combine to make the plate a showpiece for its engraver John Vallance.

The *Encyclopaedia's* legacy was shared not only by the literate public but by the Philadelphia book industry, which, for the first time, was forced to "think big." Dobson and his work played a large part in establishing the publishing hegemony of nineteenth-century Philadelphia.

ENCYCLOPÆDIA

Philad.ᵃ Published by T.Dobson Nᵒ 41 Sᵗ 2ᵈ Street 1798.

ENCYCLOPÆDIA;

OR, A

DICTIONARY

OF

ARTS, SCIENCES,

AND

MISCELLANEOUS LITERATURE;

Conſtructed on a PLAN,

BY WHICH

THE DIFFERENT SCIENCES AND ARTS

Are digeſted into the FORM of Diſtinct

TREATISES OR SYSTEMS,

COMPREHENDING

THE HISTORY, THEORY, and PRACTICE, of each,

According to the Lateſt Diſcoveries and Improvements;

AND FULL EXPLANATIONS GIVEN OF THE

VARIOUS DETACHED PARTS OF KNOWLEDGE,

WHETHER RELATING TO

NATURAL and ARTIFICIAL Objects, or to Matters ECCLESIASTICAL,
CIVIL, MILITARY, COMMERCIAL, &c.

Including ELUCIDATIONS of the moſt important Topics relative to RELIGION, MORALS, MANNERS,
and the OECONOMY of LIFE:

TOGETHER WITH

A DESCRIPTION of all the Countries, Cities, principal Mountains, Seas, Rivers, &c.
throughout the WORLD;

A General HISTORY, *Ancient* and *Modern*, of the different Empires, Kingdoms, and States;

AND

An Account of the LIVES of the moſt Eminent Perſons in every Nation,
from the earlieſt ages down to the preſent times.

Compiled from the writings of the beſt Authors, in ſeveral languages; the moſt approved Dictionaries, as well of general ſcience as of its
particular branches; the Tranſactions, Journals, and Memoirs, of various Learned Societies, the MS. Lectures of Eminent
Profeſſors on different ſciences; and a variety of Original Materials, furniſhed by an Extenſive Correſpondence.

THE FIRST AMERICAN EDITION, IN EIGHTEEN VOLUMES, GREATLY IMPROVED.

ILLUSTRATED WITH FIVE HUNDRED AND FORTY-TWO COPPERPLATES.

VOL. I.   A——ANG

INDOCTI DISCANT, ET AMENT MEMINISSE PERITI.

PHILADELPHIA:

PRINTED BY THOMAS DOBSON, AT THE STONE HOUSE, Nᵒ 41, SOUTH SECOND STREET.
M.DCC.XCVIII.
[*Copy-Right ſecured according to law.*]

Robert Street (1796-1865)
Portrait of Howell Evans
1848
Oil on canvas, 30 x 25⅛"
(76.2 x 63.8 cm)
Atwater Kent Museum,
Philadelphia
Catalogue no. 283

In 1848, Howell Evans was the young proprietor of a print shop on Fourth Street below Chestnut, just beginning his long and successful career. The pride that he took in his spacious, well-equipped workshop, uniquely furnished with a statue of the ancient goddess of wisdom, Minerva, displayed above a type case and an exotic bird perched on a gaslight fixture, could in itself have inspired the young entrepreneur to commission this portrait. Although there is a strange disparity in the scale of the various pictorial elements, the care with which the shop equipment and the activities of the workmen are recorded, and the meticulous arrangement of paper scraps in the foreground show the talent for detail and sureness of decorative color that distinguish the work of its painter Robert Street.

Born in Germantown, Street painted a variety of historical episodes, landscapes, and still lifes and an occasional full-length portrait. But the staples of his career were the half-length portraits for which he is known today; the men characteristically are shown with ruddy complexions, dark coats, and creamily painted shirt fronts, the women with costumes often rendered in surprisingly bright colors.

Benjamin Franklin
(1705/6–1790)
Batchelors-Hall
By George Webb
1731
Folio pamphlet, 12 pages
12 x 7½" (30.4 x 19 cm)
American Philosophical
Society, Philadelphia
Catalogue no. 28

Printer, inventor, scientist, writer, politician, statesman, diplomat, and philosopher—the list of accomplishments of America's first Renaissance man seems endless. But it was Benjamin Franklin's first profession as printer that gave him the most satisfaction throughout his life. *Batchelors-Hall*, a poem by George Webb defending the activities of a group of young men and their new clubhouse on the Delaware against the suspicions of Philadelphia Quakers, was Franklin's first piece of commissioned fine printing. He personally set the type, pulled the press, and folded the finished sheets.

Few Colonial printers displayed concern for the design of the material they were producing, and as a result, most books and pamphlets had wordy and unattractive title pages with too many styles and sizes of type. The overall quality of Colonial printing was also generally poor, due to stringent economic conditions and American dependence on foreign sources for materials. In particular, American printers could not afford the best or latest type faces and, instead, purchased used fonts or older and less costly castings. But it was the lack of duplicate fonts that caused an often unattractive product because type faces were used long after they should have been replaced.

Franklin, too, faced these problems, yet he consistently turned out a better product than his fellow printers. As is readily apparent from the title page of *Batchelors-Hall*, he had to use type that had worn unevenly and had become nicked and broken. This is particularly evident in the words A POEM. The lower hairline of the E has a break in it, and the M shows signs of wear, causing an uneven registration. In addition, the bodies of the C and H in BATCHELORS-HALL have nicks, and the capital E has a tilted arm. Despite this, Franklin managed to create a clean, attractive title page with a spacious elegance uncommon in Philadelphia printing. The long rules, or lines, are unbroken and relatively straight, and the ornaments both in choice and arrangement reflect Franklin's sense of design. *Batchelors-Hall* is more than just a good piece of printing. It shows the hand of an artist.

BATCHELORS-HALL;

A *Mr J. Hamilton*

POEM.

By *GEORGE WEBB.*

Si non hic tantus fructus ostenderetur, & si ex his studiis delectatio sola peteretur; tamen ut opinor, hanc animi remissionem humanissimam ac liberalissimam judicaretis: Nam hæc studia adolescentiam alunt, senectutem oblectant. Tull. pro Archia Poetâ.

PHILADELPHIA:
Printed and Sold at the *New Printing-Office,*
MDCCXXXI. Price *One Shilling.*

Eugene Feldman
(1921-1975)
Woman No. 1
1964
Photo-process offset
lithograph, 35 x 23″ (89 x
58.4 cm)
Philadelphia Museum of
Art. Purchased: Haney
Foundation Fund.
65-43-15
Catalogue no. 496

The process of offset lithography, often in combination with photographic images, had been used extensively for commercial printing since the first decade of this century, but it was not until the 1950s that artists began to explore this medium successfully. Eugene Feldman, well known in Philadelphia as a printer, teacher, and graphic artist, pioneered the use of altered photographic imagery in his offset-lithograph prints. *Woman No. 1* is part of a series of lithographs, some in reverse, some printed in several colors, based on the same image of a nude photographed while an electric fan blew her hair out in several different directions. By means of extensive photographic enlargement and exposure variation, details of the images are subordinated to large, broadly defined forms, and tonalities are reduced to extremes of black and white. Feldman developed the expressive qualities of the tonalities, not as is customarily done during the process of making the offset printing plate, but after the plate was on the press, during printing. His method is a paradox of technique, for he employed commercial printing equipment, designed for the production of vast editions of identical impressions, to create a series of unique printed variations of one image.

Joseph Pennell
(1857-1926)
*The Trains That Come
and the Trains That Go*
1919
Etching, 10 x 11¹⁵/₁₆"
(25.4 x 29.8 cm)
Philadelphia Museum of
Art. Given by John F.
Braun. 29-61-74
Catalogue no. 442

Joseph Pennell, one of Philadelphia's best-known illustrators and most prolific printmakers, was fascinated by railroads. His evocation of the train shed of Philadelphia's Broad Street Station, at one time the largest in the world, suggests the depth of his response to this subject: "Arch upon arch and tower upon tower it piles up as fine as anything abroad . . . and when it is on a spring or fall day filled with the trains that come and that go . . . the smoke and steam that comes from them is amazing . . . half the station is steam and half power . . . but the effect is now superb . . . over all the smoke curls and swirls and the sun in the late afternoon streams in and turns the station to glory, transfigures even the commuters."

Pennell's etched image of the vast train shed, drawn on the spot, reinforces his poetic vision. He is most decisive in delineating the architectural limits of the massive interior space, and his visualization of the arched trusses and their supporting members is powerful and dramatic. His emphasis centers, however, on the towers of smoke funneling up from the locomotives. While the vague figures of the commuters deftly suggest the station's activity, they are but of passing interest to Pennell; he is more forcefully inspired by the quality of the atmosphere as he creates an impressionistic vision of this enormous space.

Jessie Willcox Smith
(1863-1935)
*He Looked Up at the
Broad Yellow
Moon . . . And Thought
That She Looked at Him*
Illustration for *The
Water Babies* by Charles
Kingsley
1916
Oil over charcoal on
illustration board, 23 x
17¹/₁₆" (58.4 x 43.3 cm)
Library of Congress,
Washington, D.C.
Catalogue no. 429 a

Written by Charles Kingsley and first published in
1863, *The Water Babies* was for earlier generations,
if not for more recent ones, a very popular children's
fairy tale. It tells of a little chimney sweep named
Tom who is turned by the fairies into one of the
water babies (those smallest water fairies whose job
it is to clean the sands and rock pools after storms).
Over the years, the story was published in a number
of editions, with illustrations by several different
artists; perhaps the most enchanting are those by
Jessie Willcox Smith, a student of Howard Pyle. In
this illustration for the edition published in 1916,
the wispy silhouette of little Tom as he stares up at
the moon and the broad, flat patterning of the leaves
show the intimate quality of her work as well as her
pleasing, decorative style.

Howard Pyle (1853-1911)
*"Then dost thou not
know why I am here?"
said the Baron*
Illustration for *Otto of
the Silver Hand*
1888
Black ink on paper, 7½ x
5⅜" (19.1 x 14.3 cm)
Delaware Art Museum,
Wilmington
Catalogue no. 367 c

Rather late in his career as an illustrator, Howard Pyle turned to teaching, first at the Drexel Institute in Philadelphia, between 1894 and 1900, and then in Wilmington, Delaware, where he lived for most of his life. His extraordinary success as a teacher and the popularity of his published illustrations had a wide and strong influence on American illustration.

Otto of the Silver Hand was written and illustrated by Howard Pyle. A medieval tale—which, as far as one knows, was Pyle's own invention—it tells of the feuds of a German baron, and of the kidnapping of his son Otto by a rival baron, who cruelly mutilates the boy. Otto is eventually rescued and rises to a position of power; the silver hand of the book's title was wrought to replace the one severed by the baron directly after the confrontation illustrated here. Pyle's ink drawings for the story are characteristic of his patterned, yet virile, decorative pen work, rich in bold contrasts of pure white areas and dense darks.

Pyle suggested the intent of his story in the book's foreword: "This tale that I am about to tell is of a little boy who lived and suffered in those dark middle ages; of how he saw both the good and the bad of men, and of how, by gentleness and love and not by strife and hatred, he came at last to stand above other men and to be looked up to by all."

Eadweard Muybridge
(1830-1904)
Animal Locomotion
(Plate 521)
1887
Collotype, 11⅜ x 10⅛"
(28.9 x 25.7 cm)
Philadelphia Museum of
Art. Given by the City of
Philadelphia Trade &
Convention Center,
Department of
Commerce. 69-135-122
Catalogue no. 363 d

Between May 1884 and January 1886, under the sponsorship of the University of Pennsylvania, Eadweard Muybridge executed an extensive series of sequential photographic studies of humans and animals in motion. The result of this immense investigation was the reproduction of these photographs in 781 collotype plates, along with a separately printed prospectus and catalogue, entitled *Animal Locomotion: An Electro-Photographic Investigation of Consecutive Phases of Animal Movements*, published in 1887. To make these extraordinary photographs, Muybridge set up banks of cameras (as many as forty-eight are known to have been used for some plates) in front of which a model ran, triggering the shutters in succession and yielding an instantaneous series of images recording a complete cycle of movement. For his male models, Muybridge chose from students, doctors, and athletes who were particularly adept in the movement at which they would be photographed. He records that his female models were "chosen from all classes of society" and that the birds and wild animals came from the Zoological Society Garden. The model of this sequence labeled "walking" (A), "ascending step" (B), "throwing disc" (C), "using shovel" (D), "using pick" (E and F), who is described as "an ex-athlete, aged about sixty," can be no other than Muybridge himself. The lasting scientific merit of *Animal Locomotion* is well recognized. But today these images transcend their original analytic intent and are appreciated purely for their aesthetic value, the expressive possibility of the body in motion and the rhythm and grace of the compositions.

Ray K. Metzker (born
1931)
PCA
1965 (negative); 1975
(print)
Silver print, 39¼ x 35¾"
(99.6 x 90.8 cm)
Philadelphia Museum of
Art. Purchased:
Philadelphia Foundation
Fund and Thomas
Skelton Harrison Fund.
75-33-1
Catalogue no. 501

Ray Metzker's *PCA,* a photographic sequence of a
changing pattern of human activity set against a
constant, defined background, stresses
graphic impact over storytelling content. The
complicated array of the pattern is its subject, not
the variety of the oddly silhouetted figures who
make up those patterns. *PCA* is meant to be viewed
first in its totality and then examined strip by strip
and segment by segment. Metzker, who
photographed this sequence at the Philadelphia
College of Art (where he teaches), has said that he
wants his sequential elements "to be presented for
simultaneous viewing like a mosaic or mural." The
size of his prints (this one is about three feet square)
certainly encourages that kind of viewing: they
demand a physical distance great enough to
comprehend the image in its entirety.

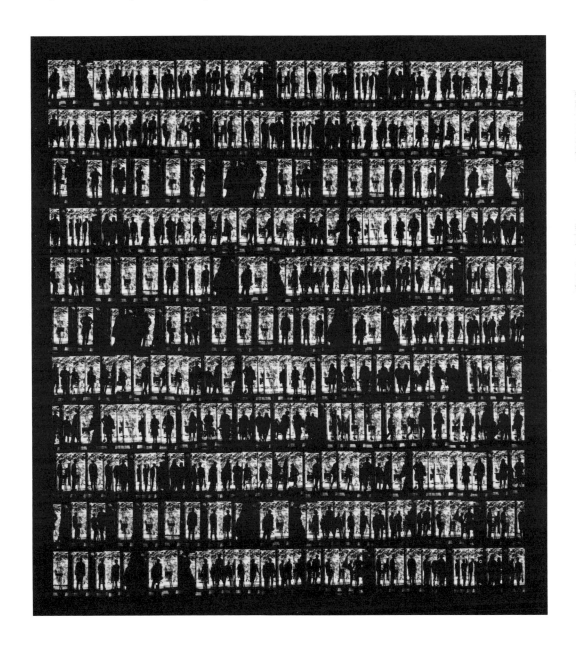

Thomas Doughty
(1793-1856)
Summer Duck (Wood Duck)
From *The Cabinet of Natural History and American Rural Sports*
Published by John Doughty
1830-33
Lithograph, 9⅜ x 11½"
(23 x 29 cm)
The Library Company of Philadelphia
Catalogue no. 242

The growing interest of Americans in their native flora and fauna is witnessed by the numerous colorplate books on these subjects that began to appear at the beginning of the nineteenth century. Among the most important early contributions of American authorship and production were William Bartram's publications on the flora of North America, Alexander Wilson's study of American birds, and John and Thomas Doughty's *Cabinet of Natural History and American Rural Sports*, first published in Philadelphia in 1830. According to its prospectus, this monthly journal was to take as its subject matter "every interesting object of Natural History scattered over our widely extended continent. The representations given, shall be as perfect as possible, and always from nature, whenever it is in our power to obtain a subject to sketch from." Although the sources of its illustrations were always specified, "from nature" generally indicated that the drawing was made from a stuffed specimen, and "from life" was more often than not a caged animal in a traveling menagerie.

Thomas Doughty always composed a habitat suitable to the wildlife depicted, be it the bleak terrain where the Newfoundland dog might roam; rivers, lakes, and waterfalls for ducks and birds; or a thunderous sky every bit as threatening as the quills of the American porcupine. In this lithographic plate, subtly colored by hand, a summer duck (wood duck) rests on a branch at the edge of a river, in a rocky setting reminiscent of much of the upstate New York scenery that Doughty was so fond of sketching and painting on his travels.

John T. Bowen
(1801-1856) after John
James Audubon
(1785-1851)
*Vulpus Fulvus, Desm.
(American Red Fox)*
1846
From *The Viviparous
Quadrupeds of North
America*
1845-48
Lithograph, 21½ x 27¾"
(54.6 x 70.5 cm)
Mrs. W. Logan MacCoy
and Morris Wood. On
loan to the Philadelphia
Museum of Art
Catalogue no. 272

The Viviparous Quadrupeds of North America has long lived in the shadow of John James Audubon's more famous undertaking, *The Birds of America.* Yet it is an amazing publication, which ventured into an area that had not been explored—the accurate representation and scientific description of America's four-legged creatures. First planned in 1839, the large colorplates, beautifully printed by John T. Bowen (then acknowledged as America's best lithographer), did not begin to appear until 1845 and the last of the three text volumes, written by Audubon's friend and patron, the Reverend John Bachman, was not published until 1854, three years after Audubon's death.

The production of the 150 plates in the *Quadrupeds* was extremely complex. Audubon had boasted that every plate in the *Birds* was based on sketches of live specimens, a boast that, while not completely true, was almost so. He never made that claim for the *Quadrupeds,* for he had great difficulty in obtaining specimens, even during his long journeys throughout the country. He used anything he could get his hands on—animal skins, stuffed specimens in New York collections, sketches of specimens in the British Museum done by his son John—and relied on his memory as well. In several instances, he traced animal figures that he had done earlier as background elements for his bird illustrations. In spite of this he rendered the animals superbly, and generally without the stiff, ungainly poses of other early painters of animals. In this plate, one of his most successful, Audubon vividly portrays an enraged American red fox caught in a hunter's trap not far from the farms he frequently menaced.

Neil Welliver (born 1929)
Windfall
1969
Oil on canvas, 72 x 72"
(182.9 x 182.9 cm)
Harcus Krakow Rosen
Sonnabend Gallery,
Boston
Catalogue no. 506

William Trost Richards
(1833–1905)
Corner of the Woods
1864
Pencil on paper, 23¼ x
17½" (59 x 44.4 cm)
Museum of Fine Arts,
Boston. M. and M.
Karolik Collection
Catalogue no. 322

Painting Maine scenes over the last ten years from widely varying vantage points, Neil Welliver has produced vistas of remote mountains, views into a meadow with its soggy marshland, and glimpses into densely wooded forest. *Windfall* belongs to this latter category, one that has preoccupied the artist increasingly in his most recent work. The dark-green and bare gray branches of pine trees fill his canvas like latticework, with only slight gleams of blue sky and its watery reflection to suggest a sense of open air and space. After first painting a small sketch of the subject, the artist returned to the site with a large canvas and completed the full-scale painting in two weeks: "I came upon this windfall after a storm in a spot with which I was well acquainted; the area had been changed dramatically, and needed to be painted—the forest is in wild flux. It is not seen when looking at the woods, but rather when living in it."

Welliver, who studied at the Philadelphia College of Art and Yale University and now teaches painting at the University of Pennsylvania, has exerted a substantial influence on a generation of students and artists interested in painting directly from life and in a return to naturalism.

The ideal picture embraces "the inexhaustible perfection of Nature's details," wrote the English critic John Ruskin. The conscientious artist must ask, "Can my details be added to? Is there a single space in the picture where I can crowd in another thought?" In the mid-nineteenth century, the philosophy behind these remarks inspired a group of young English artists known as the Pre-Raphaelites, who, along with Ruskin, influenced much of American landscape and still-life painting in the 1850s and 1860s. William Trost Richards in his *Corner of the Woods,* a broad view of an edge of a woodland with a wealth of carefully delineated natural detail, executed outdoors, illustrates the impact of this dual influence.

Done in pencil, this scene is observed from corner to corner with the seemingly impersonal, unselective eye of the camera. Richards's artistic sensibilities cannot be erased entirely, however; sheer monumentality and completeness do not necessarily convince us that the artist was merely a passively recording lens. His focus wanders, for example, among the treetops and in the distance, while returning to dwell with subjective fondness on the plants clustered around the stream in the foreground. Moreover, Richards cannot disguise the fact that he loves to draw and takes pride in his pains, as he scrapes with his fingernail or smudges the strokes, using the texture of the paper to catch glints of light—techniques that call attention to the hand of the artist as surely as they attempt to mask it. The incredibly subtle range of grays produced by all this effort expresses a wealth of Pre-Raphaelite

"truth" and has a surprisingly sensuous effect. The landscape is transformed in the process of being lovingly recorded, yielding a work that is more personal perhaps than Richards recognized or intended but precisely what Ruskin had in mind.

Andrew Wyeth (born
1917)
Quaker Ladies
1956
Dry brush and watercolor
on paper, 13¾ x 22″ (34.9
x 55.9 cm)
The Henry Francis
du Pont Winterthur
Museum, Winterthur,
Delaware.
Catalogue no. 487

Martha Mayer Erlebacher
(born 1937)
Hawkweed and Pinecone
1973
Watercolor on paper, 22 x
13" (55.9 x 33 cm)
Provident National Bank
Collection, Philadelphia
Catalogue no. 522

Quaker Ladies is one of Andrew Wyeth's most delightful works in watercolor: a panoramic view of spring compressed within a few square feet of earth sprayed with delicate star-shaped flowers. Few artists of this century have peered with such attentive eyes at the ground beneath their feet. Wyeth's landscapes are strewn with rocks and leaves and dry grasses; the minutiae of a sandbank or hillside attract his gaze far more frequently than the billowing grandeur of clouds overhead. Usually preferring to paint the bare bones of a landscape in fall or winter, rather than its summer abundance, Wyeth is somewhat sparing with floral subjects. In this watercolor, however, his work is lavish with the diminutive flowers known as Quaker Ladies (or bluets). Wyeth's skill as a watercolorist is extraordinary, and his artistry makes us oblivious of his own hand, which is everywhere at work, flicking tiny specks and dashes of color across the sheet of paper until the entire surface is as alive with his markings as the rich brown soil is alive with new growth.

Hawkweed and Pinecone, one of a group of plant studies that Martha Erlebacher has painted over the last five years, reveals her love of specific and fine detail. She spotted this particular cluster of leaves and delicate flowers in a field in the summer of 1973, and carefully carried it back to her studio; watering the hawkweed faithfully, she preserved it for several days while she completed her meticulous study of it. This watercolor is much closer in artistic intent to the sixteenth-century watercolor studies of plants and animals by Albrecht Dürer than to Andrew Wyeth's *Quaker Ladies.* Wyeth's watercolor calls the senses into play—one recalls the scent of damp soil and the rustle of spring wind; the microscopic realism of *Hawkweed and Pinecone,* on the other hand, conveys the essence of a plant rather than its physical presence.

Horace Pippin
(1888–1947)
Holy Mountain II
1944
Oil on canvas, 22 x 30″
(55.9 x 76.2 cm)
Private Collection
Catalogue no. 479

In his series of "Holy Mountain" paintings, done in the 1940s, Horace Pippin found a consoling antidote for the painful memory of World War I (in which he was severely wounded) and for his distress over the repeated horrors of World War II. His treatment of this idyllic subject combines a literal interpretation of the words of the Old Testament prophet Isaiah with images of the "Peaceable Kingdom" borrowed from the nineteenth-century Pennsylvania painter Edward Hicks. Pippin scrupulously includes all the creatures mentioned in the biblical verses (Isaiah 11:6–9)—the leopard lying down with the kid, the lion munching straw like the ox, the cow feeding with the bear, the wolf with the lamb—but he takes a delightful artistic liberty by adding three bright-green long-tailed parrots. Also prominent in Pippin's vision are the children of whom the prophet speaks: a little boy crawling toward the "hole of the asp," a girl in her best yellow polka-dotted dress playing with a doll on the "cockatrice' den," and a childlike shepherd. An affinity to Hicks's paintings is undeniable, particularly in the compositional device of clustering the animals together before a background of dense green foliage and in the wonderful sprawling pose of the leopard. The artist's lingering memory of World War I is suggested in the tiny gray bombs seen falling behind the branches at the upper left and the ominous brown figures of a hanged man and the soldiers lurking among the tree trunks.

Thomas Landon Davies
(born 1943)
Hebrides Cow
1972
Gold-toned silver print,
7 x 7" (17.7 x 17.7 cm)
Thomas L. Davies,
Berwyn, Pennsylvania
Catalogue no. 519

Hebrides Cow represents a return to more traditional pictorial imagery among contemporary photographers not unlike today's renewed interest in naturalism among painters. In its picturesque subject matter and the golden tone of the original, it is reminiscent of turn-of-the-century photographs, and its technique conforms to the standards of "purism" of that era—textures and forms are sharply seen, and defined with a precision that can be achieved only in a contact print with a large-format negative (here somewhat cropped). Although the subject might appear nostalgic, the bizarre viewpoint and posture of the cow clearly distinguish the photograph as a work of this decade.

Autograph Quilt
1842–43
Cotton chintz, satin,
brocade, and chiffon silk;
97¼ x 127¼" (247 x
323 cm)
Philadelphia Museum of
Art. Given by five
granddaughters of Samuel
Padgett Hancock: Mrs.
Levis Lloyd Mann, Mrs.
H. Maxwell Langdon,
Mrs. George K. Helbert,
Mrs. Nelson D. Warwick,
Mrs. Granville B.
Hopkins. 45-35-1
Catalogue no. 271

Appliqué was as popular as patchwork for decorating quilts in the nineteenth century, and both of these techniques were effectively combined in this large autograph quilt. Like most autograph quilts, this one was probably made to honor a special occasion, the marriage of Samuel Padgett Hancock and Charlotte Gillingham on February 22, 1844. Each colorful square contains a different design, framing a signature, which is embellished in ink with tiny sprigs and figures. "Samuel P. Hancock 1843" occupies a central square, and Charlotte's name is featured, somewhat less prominently, in a square to the left. Samuel's name is surrounded by an elaborately embroidered floral wreath; his wife's, by a finer wreath and inked doves and foliage. Because much of the same fabric is used throughout, the quilt was probably made by only one person and then passed on to others for their individual mark.

Most of the autographs are of relatives of Charlotte and Samuel and the accompanying dates are 1842 and 1843, just prior to their marriage.

Frank Furness
(1839–1912)
Elevation of Desk
About 1875
Pencil on paper, 7¹¹/₁₆ x
11⅛″ (20 x 28.2 cm)
Philadelphia Museum of
Art. Given by George
Wood Furness. 74-224-3
Catalogue no. 343 a

Frank Furness's ornamental designs had their basis in natural forms, especially leaves and flowers. His sketch books are filled with carefully detailed drawings of flowers, animals, and landscapes, all taken directly from nature. But his use of these organic forms in architecture and in this design for a monumental desk saw their transformation into boldly abstracted, ornamental motifs.

Many of the elements that give the desk its forceful architectonic quality are seen in Furness's buildings. Its three-part composition is not unlike the organization of the facade of the Pennsylvania Academy of the Fine Arts, while the Moorish arch framing the kneehole appears in several other

Furness buildings of the 1870s. The finished walnut desk, which Furness made for his brother, the noted Shakespearean scholar Horace Howard Furness, is also in the collection of the Philadelphia Museum of Art.

Dentzel Carousel
Company (1867-1928)
Carousel Figures
1903-9
Painted basswood and
taxidermist eyes; pig
height 64″ (162.5 cm),
ostrich height 77¾″
(197.4 cm)
Abby Aldrich Rockefeller
Folk Art Collection,
Williamsburg, Virginia
Catalogue no. 405

The first merry-go-rounds in Philadelphia were built
in the eighteenth century, and amusement parks
with carousels were well established by the 1860s,
when steam power became widely available. These
fanciful carousel figures are some of the best that
the Dentzel Carousel factory in Germantown
produced. Animals such as this prancing ostrich and
leaping pig were carved by Salvatore Cernigliano, an
immigrant Italian woodcarver employed by Dentzel.
Other charming mounts attributed to Cernigliano
include a cat grasping a fish in his mouth, a hopping
rabbit, and a five-foot-tall dog. Most American
carousel figures are so elaborately carved only the
on right side of the animal, whereas their left flank
was more plain since it was not readily visible when
the merry-go-round turned.

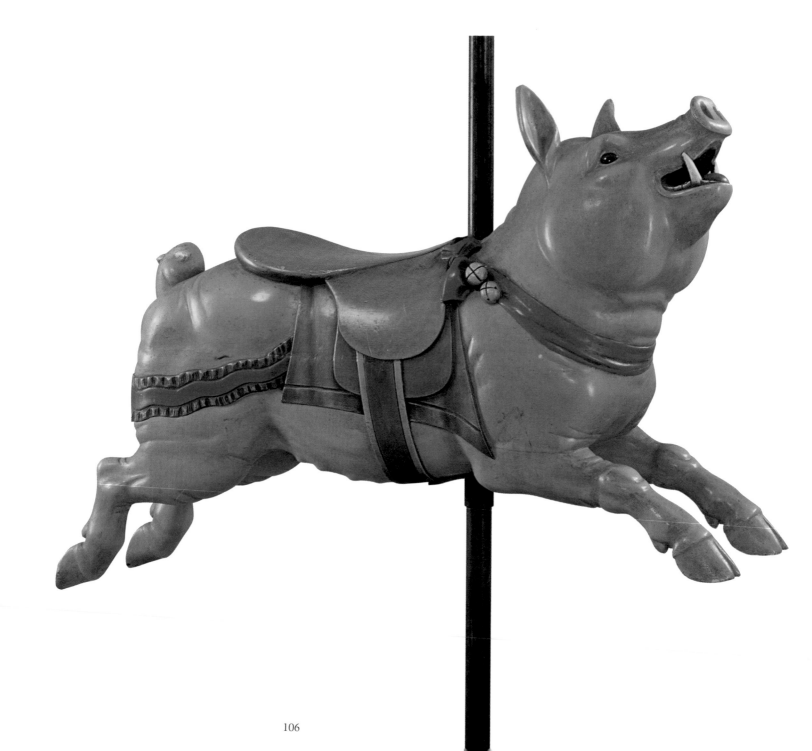

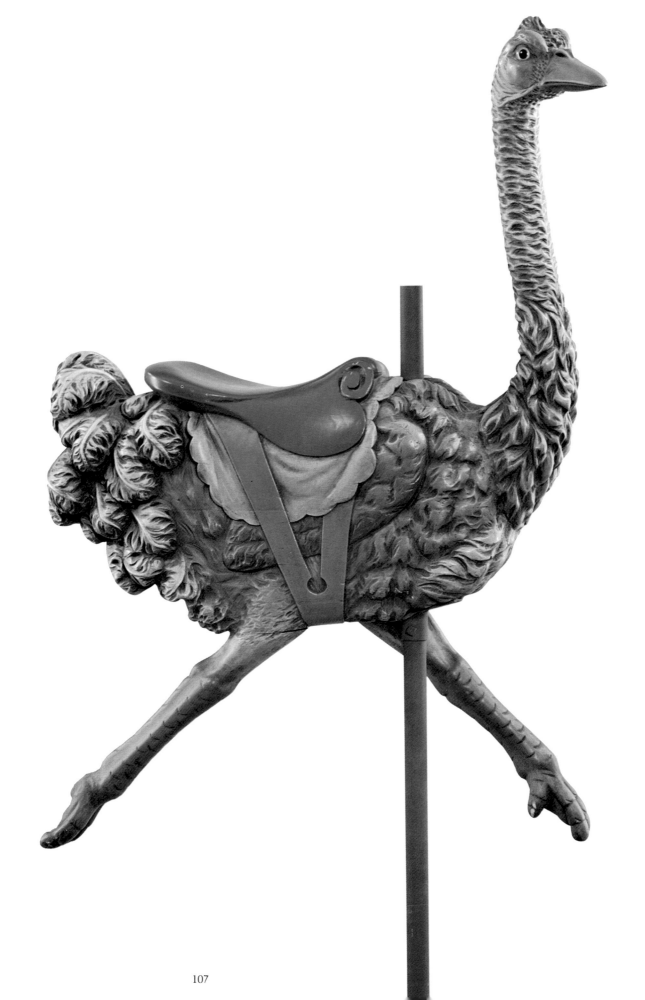

George Cochran Lambdin
(1830-1896)
Flowers in a Vase
1875
Oil on canvas, 24⅛ x
20¼" (61.2 x 51.4 cm)
Private Collection
Catalogue no. 341

George Cochran Lambdin painted floral still lifes more and more frequently as his career progressed, often choosing his subjects from the extensive garden of his Germantown home. His flower paintings became tremendously popular, and chromolithographs of them were published and widely distributed. When Lambdin died at age sixty-six, he was the leading still-life artist in Philadelphia and the most famous flower painter of his era.

The simple presentation of *Flowers in a Vase* emphasizes the individual form and character of the flowers and their vivid colors in bright light. The intense effect of direct observation was new to American painting of the 1870s, and it showed an emphasis that was different from the linear precision of earlier botanical illustration. Lambdin renders the delicately articulated, drooping structure of a fuchsia and the subtle color variations in the petals of a white rose with direct, sure strokes of pure color. In this abundant bouquet appealing directly to the senses, the particular shapes and textures and the varied reds, whites, pinks, and blues of peonies, roses, iris, phlox, fuchsia, and honeysuckle are placed against each other to highlight the individual qualities of each flower.

William Allbright (born
about 1795)
Camellia Japonica
From *The Floral
Magazine and Botanical
Repository*
1832–34
Hand-colored lithograph,
11⅛ x 8⅞" (28.3 x
22.5 cm)
The Library Company of
Philadelphia
Catalogue no. 244

Among the earliest magazines to be printed by
lithography in America, *The Floral Magazine and
Botanical Repository* first appeared in July 1832. Six
issues, each with hand-colored lithographic plates of
exotic flowers, such as this one of the *Camellia
japonica*, and of citrus plants, were published at
irregular intervals until the fall of 1834. *The Floral
Magazine* followed the format and content of
botanical periodicals published in London, which
had widespread currency in America. Its principal
innovation, besides the use of lithography, was the
inclusion of hints for cultivation. It was a magazine
aimed at an audience less interested in strictly
botanical information than the more
science-oriented British gardener. The plates were
also more ornamental in their design than the
engravings in the British magazines, which
frequently showed anatomical details and cross
sections. *The Floral Magazine* was further enhanced
by the adaptability of its finely detailed illustrations
for copying and decorative needlework.

Tucker and Hemphill
China Factory (1826–38)
Vase
About 1835
Decorated by Thomas
Tucker
Porcelain with ormolu
handles, height 21²/₃″
(55.2 cm)
Philadelphia Museum of
Art. Purchased: Joseph E.
Temple Fund. 16-185
Catalogue no. 251

As the Tucker factory's chief designer and decorator, Thomas Tucker created the lavish polychrome floral patterns for which Tucker porcelains became known. He extravagantly combined roses, tulips, daisies, wildflowers, and forget-me-nots in painted garlands and bouquets. Although botanical prints were usually the main design source for porcelain decorators, some of his floral motifs were taken directly from nature.

While freely painted, the floral bouquets on this tall vase are contained within a classical framework of ornamental gilded and salmon-colored bands. The urn, with its square base in imitation of French vases, is further ornamented with extraordinary gilded bronze handles. The use of attached metal handles was a common practice in France, especially at the Sèvres porcelain factory, in the early

nineteenth century. The Tucker factory, which had been established to supply the American market with native porcelain in the style of European wares, utilized this same device in its most elaborate pieces.

Side Chair
About 1810
Mahogany and inlay,
height 36" (91.4 cm)
Mr. and Mrs. George M.
Kaufman, Norfolk,
Virginia
Catalogue no. 174

This side chair was part of a large suite of
mahogany furniture, which included three other
side chairs as well as four matching arm chairs and
a settee that now grace the White House. The
elaborate carving—ribbons, plumes, leaf and floral
motifs—is probably based on English designs, for the
turned legs with their acanthus leafage reproduce
elements from a plate in Thomas Sheraton's
*Appendix to the Cabinet-Maker and Upholsterer's
Drawing-Book*, published in London in 1804.
Although decorative motifs similar to the vase and
flowers seen in the oval back panel appear also on
other chairs of this period, they were generally
painted on rather than so delicately inlaid with
wood of a contrasting color.

Newbold Hough Trotter
(1827-1898)
Mischief—Cat and
Workbox
1858
Oil on canvas, 19½ x 24"
(49.5 x 60.9 cm)
Private Collection
Catalogue no. 311

In this delightful work, Newbold H. Trotter, known for his paintings of animals, captures the indignant surprise of his well-fed and pampered house cat startled in an act of mischief. Both the culprit and the overturned workbox are painted in strong colors against a neutral brown background, and the red table cover provides a fine contrast for the still-life composition of brightly colored needle packets, threads, a strawberry sewing cushion, hooks, and other domestic tools, all closely observed and painted in careful detail. The blue ribbon around the cat's neck adds a particularly charming color accent.

Mischief—Cat and Workbox is simple and unpretentious in contrast to the more ambitious, sentimental, and melodramatically titled works for which Trotter was noted later in his career, such as *They Know Not the Voice of Strangers*, with its flock of sheep shrinking from sheep stealers, or *Signs of Invasion*, showing an elk discovering the debris of a lumber camp.

Lucy Catherine Zeigler
Hicks
Lap Quilt
About 1876
Silk, velvet, and satin
patches, 77^{15}/$_{16}$ x
64^{15}/$_{16}$" (198 x 165 cm)
Philadelphia Museum
of Art. Given by
Ralph T.K. Cornwell.
46-8-1
Catalogue no. 348

Another mischievous cat bedecked with a blue ribbon can be found on this quilt—along with a deer; at least ten different species of birds, some in trees with their nests and their young; a spider, several butterflies, and a number of other insects; and an abundance of clearly identifiable flowers. These motifs were all embroidered with great patience on randomly chosen and arranged patches of deep-toned velvet, silk, and satin fabric. A patchwork lap quilt such as this one was generally used in the Victorian parlor rather than in the bedroom, and it was popularly known as a "crazy" quilt after its boldly irregular patchwork design.

Albert Laessle
(1877-1954)
Billy
1914
Bronze, height 24¼"
(62.2 cm)
National Collection of
Fine Arts, Smithsonian
Institution, Washington,
D.C. Gift of the heirs of
Albert Laessle
Catalogue no. 424

Billy is surely the best-loved and most endearing outdoor sculpture in Philadelphia. A cast of this statue by Albert Laessle has stood in Rittenhouse Square since 1919, and daily visits and years of vigorous riding by flocks of children have worn and polished his back and horns (and severed the bronze tether rope, which survives in this version). Since Laessle worked exclusively from the living model, one can imagine the disruptions of studio routine caused by Billy's presence, for every bronze hair on this animal's hide bristles with mischief. Laessle's thorough knowledge of animal anatomy is tempered by a humorous sense of the goat's personality so that his carefully detailed realism is infused with a lifelike spirit and a touch of fantasy.

Wharton Esherick
(1887–1970)
Cheeter (Horse A)
1934
Painted white oak,
height 52" (132.1 cm)
The Wharton Esherick
Museum, Paoli,
Pennsylvania
Catalogue no. 463

Cheeter was long the eminently ridable delight of children when this horse and its mate *Jeeter* stood as guardians and mascots at the Hedgerow Theater in Rose Valley, Pennsylvania. The three-legged *Cheeter* sports a generous, flowing tail, while the two-legged *Jeeter* (painted bright yellow) carries his tail pointed upward at a jaunty angle. Wharton Esherick, a fine craftsman whose furniture was generally carved with exquisite precision, here left deliberate traces of his tools in the rough-hewn wood. Eliminating all but the most rudimentary details, he allowed the form of the horse to emerge only partially from the contours of the wooden tree trunk, and the tension between the wood and the image within brings the sculpture vividly to life. *Cheeter* seems to belong to the same popular branch of the animal kingdom as the sprightly horses that grace carousels and weather vanes. Esherick rarely came closer to being a true "folk" artist than in this merry animal whose apparent, yet sophisticated, crudeness only adds to its appeal.

Andrew Hamilton (1676–1741) and Edmund Woolley (about 1695–1771)
The State House (Independence Hall)
Chestnut Street, between Fifth and Sixth streets
1732–48, tower 1750–53, steeple 1828
Brick structure, granite detailing, wood trim
Catalogue no. 30

Represented by:
Matthew Albert Lotter (1741–1810)
Elevation of the State House
From *A Plan of the City and Environs of Philadelphia*
1777
Engraving, 32¼ x 26¼" (81.9 x 66.6 cm)
Private Collection

By the mid-eighteenth century, Philadelphia was in effect, if not in fact, the capital of the Colonies. At the political center of the city was the State House, designed in 1732 and still under construction in 1735, when it first housed a meeting of the Provincial Assembly. Quite typical of the way important eighteenth-century buildings were designed, the State House emerged from a collaboration of two men, a gentleman-architect and an architect-builder. Andrew Hamilton, a lawyer and member of the State House building committee, set down the initial scheme. But it was the builder, Edmund Woolley, who translated the concept into detailed drawings and who, together with his carpenter Ebenezer Tomlinson, was in charge of the numerous craftsmen employed on its construction.

The State House was initially conceived not with its commanding tower but with a more modest cupola designed simply to support a bell. The lofty steeple was added later, from 1750 to 1753, but within thirty years had fallen into such disrepair that it was removed. What we see today is a reconstruction of that steeple by the architect William Strickland.

There is no doubt that by 1750, when the Philadelphia map on which this 1777 engraving is based first appeared, the State House had already achieved recognition as an important symbol of Philadelphia. But later, as the site of the signing of the Declaration of Independence, it became a more universal symbol of freedom. With its Liberty Bell, Independence Hall—as it was first called in 1824—has served for two hundred years as an icon for all Americans.

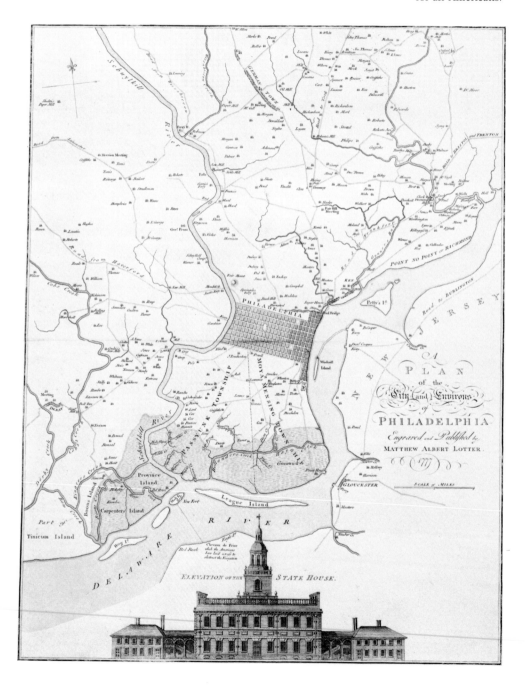

William Kneass
(1780/81–1840) after John
Hills (active 1777?–1817)
*Map of Philadelphia and
Environs*
About 1810–12
Hand-colored engraving,
39¾ x 39½" (101 x 100.7
cm)
Historical Society of
Pennsylvania,
Philadelphia
Catalogue no. 177

Centre Square, the heart of William Penn's grid plan for his "greene countrie town," forms the focal point for this spectacular circular map of Philadelphia, engraved about 1810–12. Showing an area radiating ten miles in all directions from Centre Square, the map had little pretense at utility; rather it was made to have aesthetic appeal for Philadelphia's wealthy citizens, whose country estates are clearly indicated in the city's environs.

Aptly chosen to symbolize Philadelphia in its second century was the city's latest technical marvel, the classical Centre Square Pump House shown at the bottom left. Water was pumped from the Schuylkill through a covered brick tunnel to Centre Square, and from there distributed by a gravity-feed system through wooden pipes to sixty-three private homes, four breweries, and a sugar refinery.

The figures shown in front of the Pump House represent Science instructing Youth in the Fine Arts. The group at the right of the map glorifies the benefits of Peace, Commerce, Agriculture, Fishing, and Industry. Benjamin Henry Latrobe, the architect of the Pump House, had expressed hope that Philadelphia might one day become the Athens of America. However, one suspects that John Hills was much closer to the mark in suggesting through these allegorical scenes that Philadelphia's future depended not upon the arts so much as upon trade, industry, and science.

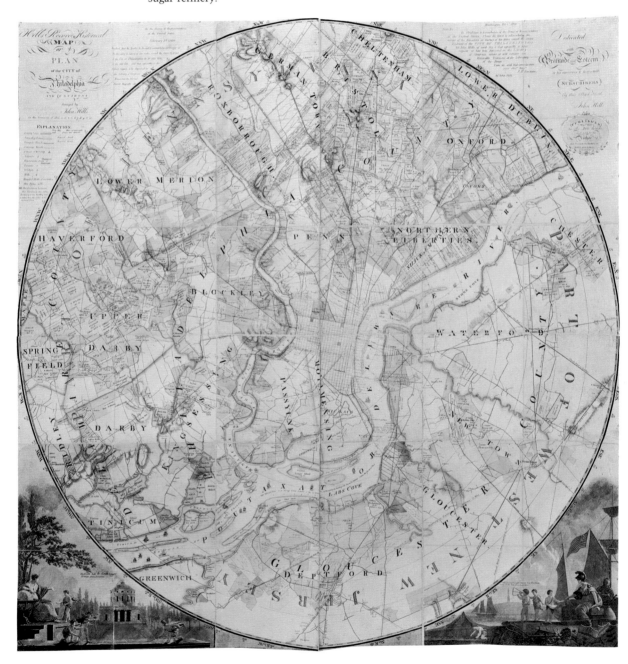

John Kearsley (1684–1772) and Robert Smith (1722–1777)
Christ Church
Second Street, above Market Street
1727–44, steeple 1752–54
Brick structure, granite water table, stone detailing, wood trim, iron gates and railing
Catalogue no. 26

Represented by:
William Strickland (1788–1854)
Christ Church
1811
Oil on canvas, 48 x 52" (122 x 132 cm)
Historical Society of Pennsylvania, Philadelphia

"They are bringing the priest and the sword among us," cried the Quakers when the Anglican community sought ground for the first Christ Church in 1694. The first buildings of Christ Church and the Great Meeting, a block away at Second and High (Market) streets, were begun at the same time and progressed at the same pace. The Meeting House was a large structure of brick; Christ Church, a smaller building of wood. By 1726, the congregation had outgrown the first church, and the following year a new brick building was begun. Completed in 1744, the second Christ Church would remain the most elaborate and highly ornamented building in the city until construction of City Hall some 150 years later.

William Strickland's view of the east end of the church emphasizes its imposing scale in comparison with the adjoining shops and houses and its ambitious architectural design, based on churches by the English architect Sir Christopher Wren as well as on architectural design books. The great three-part Palladian window, which illuminates the chancel end, dominates the east facade, also elaborated with white wood cornices and moldings, medallions, scrolls, and urns. The steeple, constructed in 1754 by the architect Robert Smith, is topped with a bishop's miter weather vane added about 1787–94.

Pavel Petrovitch Svinin
(1787/88-1839)
*Sunday Morning in Front
of the Arch Street
Meeting House,
Philadelphia*
1811-13
Watercolor over pencil
on paper, 9 x 7⁵/₁₆"
(22.9 x 18.2 cm)
The Metropolitan
Museum of Art, New
York. Rogers Fund, 1942
Catalogue no. 182 c

The diversity of religious expression in the United States both interested and appalled Pavel Petrovitch Svinin, a Russian amateur artist who served as secretary to the Russian consul-general in Philadelphia from 1811 to 1813. Although critical and even derisive of most American religious sects, Svinin respected the Quakers and praised them for their honesty and charity. To their influence he attributed the "deep silence and quiet" of Sundays in Philadelphia. "On these days, in the streets of Philadelphia one meets only the somber faces of people deep in meditation; one cannot see one smile, as if the whole city were in mourning." In *Sunday Morning*, Svinin depicts a mild clash between the older, austere Quaker mores and the newer, less restrained conduct and fashions that were gradually appearing. On the sidewalk outside the Arch Street Meeting House, erected by the Quakers between 1803 and 1811, a plainly dressed family representing the old order unexpectedly comes upon two fashionably clad young ladies. As the boy reaches out for the yellow butterfly that floats, appropriately, before the young women, the father restrains him and scowls fiercely at this breach of established religious decorum.

George Heap (about
1715–1752)
with Nicholas
Scull (1687–1761)
*An East Prospect of the
City of Philadelphia*
1754
Engraving, four plates,
each 21¼ x 20⅛" (54 x
51.1 cm)
The Episcopal Academy,
Merion, Pennsylvania
Catalogue no. 46

"Philadelphia will make a most miserable
Perspective for want of steeples." This was the
answer to Pennsylvania Proprietor Thomas Penn's
request from London for a view of the city in 1750.
Midcentury Philadelphia still revealed its Quaker
heritage in its lack of steeples, which were
considered an unnecessary ornament for Quaker
Meeting Houses. However, by the time the view
was finally undertaken in 1752, two additional
steeples had been projected—those of Christ Church
and the State House (Independence Hall)—and by
the time it was engraved in 1754, both had been
completed. Drawn most likely from the architects'
elevations, these steeples add greatly to the variety
of Philadelphia's skyline.

The most notable characteristic of Philadelphia's Colonial architecture was its homogeneity. Most of the earliest English inhabitants of the city had lived through the Great Fire of London in 1666 and had seen the style of its rebuilding, credited to Sir Christopher Wren. William Penn had cautioned about fire at the outset of Philadelphia's settlement in 1682 and hoped to minimize that hazard, as well as other Old World ills, by spacing buildings and surrounding them, at least the domestic structures, with orchards and gardens. Had the town spread evenly across its site to the Schuylkill as Penn envisioned, there would have been room for his dream of a "greene countrie town"; however, Heap's view shows clearly that mercantile opportunity erased the memory of past catastrophes and that the prosperity of the second generation in Philadelphia determined its architectural growth.

It is difficult to visualize the eighteenth-century visitor's impression of neatness and order, but compared to Boston and New York, which grew without preconceived plans, and Newport, constructed mostly of wood, Philadelphia was quite advanced. It was built by craftsmen trained in the environs of London. The plain, rectangular shape of the brick buildings, with gable, hip, and occasionally gambrel roofs, prominent hooded doorways, white stone belt courses, balustrades, and white wooden sash windows were all common elements of English town architecture. Small houses in London and Bristol served as models for Philadelphia builders, who used the same design books as their English counterparts.

In 1765, Lord Adam Gordon from Aberdeenshire, Scotland, who visited most of the larger cities on the east coast of America, reserved his highest praise for Philadelphia: "The city of Philadelphia is perhaps one of the wonders of the world, if you consider its size, the number of inhabitants, the regularity of its streets, their great breadth and length, their cutting [one] another all at right angles, their spacious public and private buildings, quays and docks, the magnificence and diversity of places of worship, the plenty of provisions brought to market, and the industry of all its inhabitants. One will not hesitate to call it the first town in America, but one that bids fair to rival almost any one in Europe."

Paul P. Cret (1876-1945),
Horace Trumbauer
(1868-1938), C. Clark
Zantzinger (1872-1954)
and others
*Benjamin Franklin
Parkway*
Design begun 1907
Catalogue no. 411

Represented by:
Jacques Gréber
(1882-1962)
*Plan of the Benjamin
Franklin Parkway*
About 1917
Watercolor and ink on
paper; left section 55⅜ x
111⅝" (140.6 x 283.5
cm), right section 55⅜ x
107¾" (140.6 x 273.6 cm)
Philadelphia Museum of
Art

In 1682, Thomas Holme was retained by William
Penn to lay out the city of Philadelphia, which
would stretch between the Schuylkill and Delaware
rivers. With no important man-made structures and
few land formations of any consequence to affect his
design, Holme turned to an abstraction, a rectilinear
grid of streets, quartered by two principal avenues,
Broad and High (now Market) streets, which
intersected at Centre Square (now Penn Square).
Public squares were planned in the center of each
quadrant, thus reflecting in each quarter the overall
totality of the city.

For the small-scale pedestrian city of the eighteenth
and the early nineteenth century, the original plan
remained adequate. Its limits became evident at the
end of the nineteenth century, when the increasing
sprawl of the city, rapid commercial growth, and an

insatiable demand for speed caused city leaders to look for alternatives. In 1891, spurred by the example of Baron Haussmann's broad avenues in Paris, a gigantic diagonal boulevard was proposed, joining Penn Square with Logan Square and continuing to Twenty-fourth and Callowhill streets. This would link center city to the remnant of Penn's "greene countrie town"—Fairmount Park. A decade later, in 1901, the scheme again came to the fore; however, there was great debate about the design and route of the parkway, and despite the support of the press and the city government, it progressed slowly.

Several years later, in 1907, Paul P. Cret, Horace Trumbauer, and C. Clark Zantzinger were employed as associate architects to draw up another scheme for the parkway. Their proposal, a grand boulevard passing from City Hall to Logan Square and on to the Fairmount reservoir, presented an axial, formal arrangement, with City Hall at one end, and at the other, on Fairmount, an imposing new art museum. But the parkway was designed to be more than an express route to the park, and a vista to City Hall. The architects also anticipated that it would become the site of the principal buildings of the city, spurring economic development of the region. The lower parkway would contain new commercial buildings, offices, hotels, and stores. Logan Square, as is evident on the right of Gréber's plan, would be reserved for public institutions—the public library, the county courthouse, the Franklin Institute, and the department of education—which would join the Cathedral of SS Peter and Paul and the Academy of Natural Sciences.

The remainder of the parkway would be the site of a new Episcopal Cathedral (center bottom), twin buildings for the Pennsylvania Academy of the Fine Arts and a new Museum School of Industrial Arts, in addition to the ambitious Philadelphia Museum of Art (left). Only the last of these originally planned structures was constructed, begun in 1919 and first opened to the public in 1928, although it was joined in 1929 by Paul P. Cret's diminutive gem, the Rodin Museum.

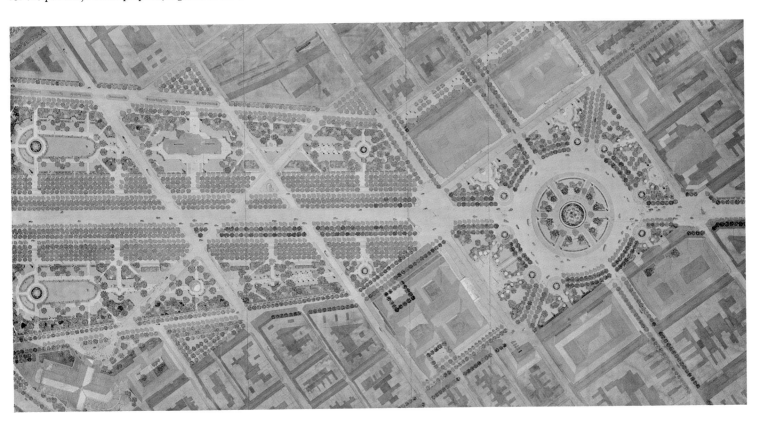

Gustavus Hesselius
(1682-1755)
Lapowinsa
1735-37
Oil on canvas, 33 x 25"
(83.3 x 63.5 cm)
Historical Society of
Pennsylvania,
Philadelphia
Catalogue no. 31

Lapowinsa was one of the Delaware Indian chiefs who on May 9, 1735, tentatively agreed to the Walking Purchase Treaty, concluded in 1737. To settle a land controversy, John and Thomas Penn, sons of William Penn, suggested that the colonists be granted as much Indian land as could be walked across in a day and a half—about 25 miles by Indian standards. Unknown to the Indians, the Penns had sold thousands of acres of the disputed land as early as 1728; and when the day of the infamous "walk" arrived in 1737, the Penns used expert hikers and a carefully surveyed, predetermined route. The result was that the walkers averaged nearly 3¾ miles per hour and covered about 60 miles in the designated time.

This portrait of Lapowinsa seems to have been painted just after the Walking Purchase agreement, well before the actual "walk." It is believed that the portrait was commissioned by the Penns, possibly as a token of friendship with the Indians, and may even have been begun on May 9, 1735, in commemoration of the initial agreement. Lapowinsa's head, so sympathetically conceived, has the honesty and freshness of a portrait from life, whereas the smoother and more meticulous painting of the body suggests that it is a later and somewhat idealized addition by its Swedish-born artist, Gustavus Hesselius.

Alexander Milne Calder
(1846–1923)
Model for the Statue of
William Penn
1886
Bronze, height 28″
(71.1 cm)
Mr. and Mrs. Set Charles
Momjian, Huntingdon
Valley, Pennsylvania
Catalogue no. 369

Philadelphia's best-known landmark, the statue of William Penn on top of the tower of City Hall, is Alexander Milne Calder's major work, the one on which his reputation was built. Calder based his naturalistic depiction of William Penn holding the Charter of Pennsylvania on thorough research. For example, the Historical Society of Pennsylvania was commissioned to investigate the kind of costume Pennsylvania's first Proprietor would have worn, and Calder himself carefully studied Benjamin West's painting of *Penn's Treaty with the Indians* to capture William Penn "as he is known to Philadelphians." Because of the great distance from which the statue would be viewed, Calder strove to interpret Penn in a broad, highly legible way. However, he later claimed that this effect was not achieved because the statue was faced toward the northeast, in the direction of the Treaty Tree in Kensington, with the features thrown into shadow, while Calder had intended the face to be etched in bold relief by light from the south.

The enlargement of the figure from the original three-foot-high model approved in 1886 to the twenty-six-ton statue completed in 1892 occupied Calder almost exclusively for six years. A number of bronze casts such as this one were taken from the earliest plaster model, evidently intended as souvenirs or ornaments. To produce the full-size version, a thirty-six-foot-high clay model was first made, painstakingly built up on an iron and wood framework; a plaster replica, constructed in sections, was undertaken next and finished by August 1888. But the figure immediately became a victim of its own size, for there was no American bronze foundry that could cast such an enormous work until Philadelphia's Tacony Iron and Metal Works was established a year and a half later. The fourteen sections of the bronze statue were finally assembled in the courtyard of City Hall in November 1892, and the statue remained on view there for two years. In 1894, *William Penn* was hoisted onto the tower where it remains as the highest point in the city and a well-loved citizen of Philadelphia.

Earl Horter (1883–1940)
City Hall: Philadelphia
About 1920
Pencil on paper, 19½ x
14″ (49.5 x 35.6 cm)
Philadelphia Museum of
Art. Purchased:
Haney Foundation Fund.
72-25-1
Catalogue no. 445

Earl Horter's vision of the 548-foot tower of
Philadelphia's City Hall gives ample evidence of his
brilliance as a draftsman, as well as his ability to
absorb styles and techniques from other artists. By
1920, Horter was thoroughly familiar with the
formal innovations of the cubists and their
colleagues in Paris, as is suggested by the style of
this drawing. Indeed, Horter would eventually play
an important role in introducing modern art to
Philadelphia, not only as an artist and teacher but
also as a discerning collector. Horter has chosen to
view City Hall from South Broad Street, where
neighboring buildings provide the tower with a tall,
narrow frame of architectural elements. Fragmented
sky and solid forms interpenetrate, and the whole
scene takes on an aura of rapid motion. To guide the
viewer through this disjointed space, familiar details
remain, including the statue of William Penn, the
monumental clock (which reads 11:40), and so on
down to the lamppost by the great entrance
archway. At the foot of the building a sketchy
jumble of cars and passersby suggests a futuristic
Philadelphia rush hour.

John McArthur, Jr.
(1823-1890)
Philadelphia City Hall
Penn Square
1870-1901
Dressed and rusticated
granite blocks on ground
story; brick and iron
frame of upper stories
and tower faced with
marble ashlar
Catalogue no. 334

Represented by:
City Hall
About 1901
Chromolithograph, 27 x
22⅝" (68.5 x 57.4 cm)
INA Museum, INA
Corporation, Philadelphia

Philadelphia City Hall stands without peer, overshadowing its neighbors, dominating the skyline, and determining the design scheme of the city's business district. However, from its earliest planning stages the building was steeped in controversy, first over the choice of its architect, John McArthur, Jr., and then over its site—originally it had been planned for Independence Square. In this century, City Hall has been disdained by those with anti-Victorian sentiments, and as late as 1952, the city seriously entertained tearing it down, except for the tower which would have remained, standing in the midst of a traffic island.

City Hall was designed in the self-consciously historic French style of the Paris of Napoleon III known as the Second Empire. When McArthur began City Hall, he was following this popular and, for America, "modern" style, but by the time the building was completed in 1901, the Second Empire style was long out of date. McArthur, however, continued to direct his energy into his work to give that transitory fashion its fullest expression, and through the rich use of sumptuous sculpture, to transform the building into an encyclopedia of allegorical statements. The elaborate decorations, all designed by Alexander Milne Calder, include statues, reliefs, and panels of statesmen and early settlers and personifications of the continents, elements, seasons, and the arts. The figures on the tower carry out the theme of the founding of Pennsylvania and Philadelphia, and the entire composition is surmounted by the statue of William Penn holding the Charter of Pennsylvania.

Bold dormers enrich the mansard roofs which rise to steep peaks on each of the corners and swell into bulbous forms atop the four central pavilions. Monumental vaulted corridors lead through each heavily wrought center pavilion to a central courtyard, which remains the most heavily traveled public square in the city and one of the finest urban spaces in this country.

Venturi and Rauch,
Architects and Planners
(established 1964)
Franklin Court
314–22 Market Street
1974–76
With John Milner,
National Heritage
Corporation,
Restoration Architects
Catalogue no. 539

Represented by:
Mark Cohn
Franklin Court:
Interior Court
1976
Photograph
Courtesy Venturi
and Rauch,
Architects and Planners,
Philadelphia

Judd's Hotel,
Philadelphia
1817–25
Oil on canvas, 30 x 25″
(76.2 x 63.5 cm)
Philadelphia Museum of
Art. Collection of Edgar
William and Bernice
Chrysler Garbisch.
68-222-4
Catalogue no. 207

When the National Park Service decided to construct a new museum at the site of Benjamin Franklin's house, the firm of Venturi and Rauch was commissioned to design a different sort of historic monument, one that would present what was known about the site as well as reveal the breadth of Franklin's personality and interests.

Little remained of the original Franklin Court. It was known that a row of houses fronting on Market Street opened through an archway into a large court containing a print shop, and beyond it, Franklin's own house. Enough of the Market Street row survived to permit its accurate reconstruction, but Franklin's house and his grandson's print shop had been demolished in the early nineteenth century, making any restoration of these structures highly speculative.

Venturi and Rauch developed an original design, not initially apparent from the principal approach on Market Street. There, the first structures encountered are the reconstructed Colonial houses, which though banal, serve to announce the museum within. The view through the restored archway, however, reveals a landscaped court that is in startling contrast with the naive realism of the restored buildings: two immense tubular steel frames, shaped to the outline of corner posts, cornices, gable roofs, and chimneys, form "ghosts" (in the architects' words) of the volume but not the detail of the long-demolished house and print shop. Within the ghost frames, the architects sought to represent what little is known of the lost buildings. Slate paving indicates the floor areas, while the location of walls, partitions, and such features as fireplaces are marked by white marble slabs.

Descriptions of the house and the print shop from contemporary sources are inscribed in the paving, thereby uniting documentation with the symbolic representation. Finally, the actual remnants of the building, the foundation walls, are here and there made visible in deep, glazed viewing boxes. Beneath the entire site is a museum in which the various aspects of Franklin's life are introduced. Through its several modes of presentation of history, Franklin Court makes evident the vitality of the man it celebrates and suggests the variety of means by which the past can be made present.

This picturesque view of Philadelphia by an unknown artist catches the speeding arrival of a coach-and-four outside Judd's Hotel at 32 South Third Street. The hostelry was the terminus of the daily passenger coach route from Trenton, and the carriage in this painting was touted as "the fastest mail coach in the United States, the New York–Philadelphia express—through to each destination in one day."

Judd's Hotel captures an engaging Philadelphia scene, and in so doing gives some impression of street life and architecture of the city in the early nineteenth century. The iron framework running along the sidewalk curb was used to support awnings strung out from the building facades—a convenience that was discarded long ago.

William L. Johnston (1811-1849) and Thomas Ustick Walter (1804-1887)
Dr. Jayne's Building (Jayne Building)
84 Chestnut Street
1849-50 (demolished 1957-58)
Brick, with granite front and rear, interior iron columns and wooden girders supporting floors
Catalogue no. 285

Represented by:
John M. Butler (active 1841-after 1860)
Jayne Building
About 1850-60
Engraving, 21½ x 15⅛″
(54.6 x 38.4 cm)
The Library Company of Philadelphia

Because of its height and design, the Jayne Building, built in Philadelphia in 1850, has been widely hailed as a proto-skyscraper. When it was completed, it loomed almost one hundred feet above the city. Only a few church spires extended higher than its wooden tower, which quickly became a Philadelphia landmark and a popular point from which to view the city. While height was to become increasingly desirable with escalating commercial real estate values, here it was probably motivated more by prestige and publicity for Dr. Jayne's patent medicine factory housed within. The building's contribution to the development of modern architecture was not its height alone, but also its design and the way in which the architect adapted the verticality of the Gothic style to a tall commercial building on a narrow urban lot. By recessing the spandrels, architect William L.

Johnston was able to emphasize the verticality of the clustered columns, gracefully resolving their upward thrust by merging the vertical lines into Gothic arches and continuing them above into oculi with inset quatrefoils.

After Johnston's death in October 1849, Thomas U. Walter was called in to supervise the completion of the project. Walter was responsible for adding one story to the height and crowning the building with the blatantly symbolic mortars and pestles and the two-story castellated tower. Towers were then becoming very popular for commercial buildings, and others were soon built with the purpose of drawing the attention of the public; it could, in fact, be argued that New York's Empire State Building is a logical extension of this same concept of architectural advertising.

William E. Winner
(about 1815–1883)
Crazy Nora
About 1860–65
Oil on canvas, 24 x 18"
(61 x 45.7 cm)
Historical Society of
Pennsylvania,
Philadelphia
Catalogue no. 324

The woman well-known in Philadelphia as Crazy Nora was an Irish-born servant whose mind had become deranged in the 1820s and who spent her days on the streets. According to J.F. Watson's *Annals of Philadelphia*, however,"she was sane on many points and methodical in her ways. During the day she was continually on the tramp, and was . . . so well known that she was employed as a dun to collect difficult debts, in which employment she was indefatigable. . . . She thus supported herself almost to the day of her death . . . when she was about sixty-seven years of age. Her costume usually consisted of a not very full nor long dress, compressed at the waist with a belt and buckle; over this was worn a camlet cloak fastened at the neck, mostly of plaid material. She wore a pair of high-top boots and a man's hat—in winter a rather broad-brimmed stovepipe hat, and in summer a tall straw hat."

In contrast to the humorous and sentimental interpretations of contemporary life that William Winner painted for over four decades, his small portrait of *Crazy Nora* stands as an unidealized record of personality. Tightly painted detail and drab tones render all the hard surfaces of a Philadelphia street in the mid-nineteenth century. The unbroken row of buildings and the small, oblivious figures in the background isolate the figure of Crazy Nora in an impersonal setting, and Winner's acute perception of her isolation within herself creates a compelling portrayal of a disturbed mind.

Attributed to the Union
Flint Glass Works
(1826–44)
Tumbler
About 1830–40
Blown, cut, and engraved
glass; height 4⅜"
(11.1 cm)
Mr. and Mrs. Bertram D.
Coleman, Bryn Mawr,
Pennsylvania
Catalogue no. 252 b

The view of the Second Bank of the United States engraved on this diminutive tumbler is a faithful copy after an engraving published in C. G. Childs's *Views in Philadelphia and Its Vicinity* in 1830. When the architectural competition for this bank was announced in May 1818, the directors requested "a chaste imitation of Grecian Architecture, in its simplest and least expensive form." Their first choice was William Strickland's design, which was both simple and Grecian. Its most imposing aspect, the eight-column Doric portico, was copied directly from an engraving of the Parthenon in Athens. As one of the country's first public buildings based on a famous ancient monument, the Second Bank of the United States helped to establish the popularity of the Greek revival style, and the erection of twenty-four branch banks throughout the nation did much to spread it.

Louis Marie François
Rihouet (French, active
1818-55)
Dessert Plate
About 1840
Hard-paste porcelain,
diameter 9″ (22.8 cm)
Philadelphia Museum of
Art. Given by Mrs. John
Penn Brock. 64-115-16
Catalogue no. 266

Philadelphians had long been in the practice of adorning their dining tables with porcelain imported from England, France, and the Orient. After the Napoleonic Wars, French merchants and porcelain decorators, among them Louis Marie François Rihouet, began to reproduce American views on their tablewares to build up their business with American clients. The Philadelphia views in the Rihouet dinner service to which this dessert plate belongs were taken from the most popular engravings of the period, notably those originally published in C. G. Childs's *Views in Philadelphia and Its Vicinity* in 1830 and circulated in France in pirated editions.

This dessert plate depicts the "Museum de Philadelphie." Founded by Charles Willson Peale in 1786, the Museum was later housed on the second

floor of the State House (Independence Hall). Its most famous curiosity was, without question, the giant prehistoric mastodon skeleton that had been excavated under Peale's guidance. In 1828, the Museum was transferred to the Arcade Building on Chestnut between Sixth and Seventh streets, shown here. In its first directory advertisement taken after the move to the Arcade, the Museum was described as "the oldest and largest establishment in the United States [with] collections of the Animal and Mineral kingdoms of nature . . . of implements and ornaments of our aboriginal tribes . . . and of Portraits of American Statesmen and Warriors of the Revolution."

Henry Dawkins (active about 1753–86) and John Steeper (active 1755–62)
A South-East Prospect of Pennsylvania Hospital
1761
Engraving with watercolor, 8⅜ x 13⅞"
(21.3 x 35.2 cm)
Private Collection
Catalogue no. 59

The idea for a hospital for the sick and the insane was proposed in 1751 by Dr. Thomas Bond and promoted through the press of Benjamin Franklin. It was finally approved because of Franklin's then novel scheme of "matching funds," which solved the financial quandry of raising £4,000 to begin construction. Of it Franklin said, "I do not remember any of my political Manoeuvres, the Success of which gave me at the time more Pleasure. Or that in after-thinking of it, I more easily excus'd my-self for having made some Use of Cunning."

Pennsylvania Hospital stands today on its original site, bounded by Eighth, Ninth, Spruce, and Pine streets. At the time of this view only the east wing (on the right) had been realized. Indeed, the hospital trustees had commissioned this engraving to stimulate interest in the hospital and to raise funds for its completion. Henry Dawkins and John Steeper

were hired to engrave the plate, and although some problems with perspective were encountered, showing their lack of artistic training, their facility with engraving techniques shows that the two were skilled craftsmen.

Designed by Samuel Rhoads, Pennsylvania Hospital, with its brick construction punctuated by glazed headers, flat, keyed window arches, and stone belt course, copied the architectural style traditional in Philadelphia by midcentury. When the hospital was completed in the 1790s, Rhoads's original plan for the west wing was followed to achieve architectural balance; however, the design of the central pavilion was altered to the marble-and-brick neoclassical form we know today. The handsome circular drum was completed in 1799, enclosing the sky-lit surgical amphitheater, the first in America.

A South-East Prospect of the Pensylvania Hospital, with the Elevation of the intended Plan.
This Building, by the Bounty of the Government, And of many private Persons, Was Piously founded, for the Relief of the Sick and Miserable A Dom. 1755.
TAKE CARE OF HIM NI WILL REPAY THEE
Montgomery and Winter Del. Printed and Sold by Rob. Kennedy Philad.   J. Steeper & H. Dawkins Sculp.

Louis I. Kahn
(1901–1974)
*Alfred Newton Richards
Medical Building,
University of
Pennsylvania*
Thirty-seventh Street and
Hamilton Walk
1957–60
Pre-cast reinforced-
concrete structure,
brick sheathing,
and glass
Catalogue no. 489

Represented by:
*Richards Medical
Laboratories: Perspective
Drawing (Preliminary
Version)*
1957
Charcoal on tracing
paper, 23⅞ x 31″ (60.6 x
78.7 cm)
The Museum of Modern
Art, New York. Gift of
the Architect

When he was age four, Louis Kahn and his family emigrated from Russia to settle in Philadelphia, the city he would later suggest was "the place where a little boy walking through its streets can sense what he someday would like to be." After exploring music and painting, Kahn settled on architecture, which he studied at the University of Pennsylvania. In the 1930s and 1940s, Kahn encountered and sought to absorb concepts of European modernism, chiefly through the ideas of Le Corbusier. After nearly a generation of search and reaction against his Beaux-Arts training, Kahn began to evolve his own contribution to modern architecture: a synthesis of the structurally and functionally determined volumes derived from his academic schooling with the frank use of modern technology and materials.

In the Richards Medical Building at the University of Pennsylvania, Kahn devised an almost picturesque ensemble of laboratory towers and shaftways joined to a core of elevators, air intakes, and other mechanical services. Each different activity is evident from the exterior: laboratories at the corners of each tower are indicated by glass enclosures, and shaftways and stairs, by continuous brick sheathing, while office units project outward from the tower core. Such differentiation of form to suggest diverse activities was not new; Victorian architects, especially in Philadelphia, had long produced a sort of functional realism as a means of generating architectural form. But, in an era when slick glass curtain walls enveloped buildings totally with no hint of the activities within, Kahn's logically variegated design marked a striking departure from contemporary practice.

Nicolino (Visconte di)
Calyo (1799-1884)
View of the Waterworks
1835-36
Watercolor and gouache
on paper, 26⅛ x 36¼"
(66.3 x 92 cm)
Private Collection
Catalogue no. 257

When the city's Pump House at Centre Square proved insufficient for the expanding metropolis, a new steam-powered Waterworks was constructed from the designs of Frederick Graff. The new facility began operations in September 1815 in a stuccoed stone house on the east bank of the Schuylkill at the foot of Fairmount. Water was pumped into a reservoir atop the hill and then gravity fed to homes and hydrants. The steam engines were costly and troublesome, however, and in 1819 a shift to waterpower was begun, with a new millhouse and machinery built next to the steam-engine house. Stuccoed pavilions with Doric tetrastyle porticoes terminate each end of the millhouse; in the absence of an accepted industrial style, the use of Roman revival end pavilions was the most appropriate available, conjuring up images of Roman civilization and its famed engineering feats.

From the beginning the scenic virtues of the landscaped site were appreciated, and it became one of Philadelphia's best-known locales and a favorite promenade. Views of it were recorded in virtually every medium. Nicolino Calyo painted this watercolor view during a visit to the city about 1835 or 1836. Like most painters of his day, Calyo organized what he saw—even if he "painted on the spot" (as the inscription at the lower left records)—in terms of picturesque formulas, and felt fully licensed to rearrange appearances for the sake of artistic effect. As an accomplished professional, Calyo carried all of this off without loss of authenticity, and in fact his additional artifices—the birds on the river, the tiny figures on the banks, or the jaunty boatman, smoking and tending his teakettle—only add to the charm and interest of the scene.

Thomas Fletcher
(1787–1866)
Presentation Urn
About 1833
Silver, height 20⅛″
(51.1 cm)
Joseph Sorger,
Philadelphia
Catalogue no. 247

In 1815, the Pennsylvania legislature chartered the Schuylkill Navigation Company to construct a lock canal from Fairmount in Philadelphia to Port Carbon in Schuylkill County, a distance of about 110 miles. Designed by Ariel Cooley of Springfield, Massachusetts, the project required the construction of many dams, canals, and locks, including the dam and lock at the Fairmount Waterworks. The project took about ten years to complete and it was not until 1825 that the first boats to traverse the entire length arrived in Philadelphia. This scheme had been backed by the merchant and banker Stephen Girard, who realized the potential of the anthracite coal deposits in the interior of Pennsylvania, especially the Lehigh Valley. The company's dams also were to provide abundant waterpower, which paved the way for the development of industrial mill towns along the Schuylkill, such as Manayunk.

A project as extensive as this navigation system was achieved only with great difficulty, and it was due to the company's local managers that this speculative endeavor succeeded. As a token of appreciation, the company presented silver pieces to each of the five Philadelphia managers, including Thomas Firth, the recipient of this urn. Designed by Thomas Fletcher, a Philadelphia silversmith known for his ambitious presentation silver, the urn is based on English adaptations of the Warwick Vase, a famous classical urn excavated in 1771 from Hadrian's Villa, near Rome, and later owned by the Duke of Warwick. The panels on the sides of the square base show four different vistas along the Schuylkill. On the top, a classical figure, seated on an urn from which spills forth the Schuylkill's waters, holds a cornucopia symbolizing the benefits brought by the company's successful venture.

William Rush
(1756–1833)
The Schuylkill Freed
1825
Spanish cedar (originally
painted), length 87″
(220.9 cm)
Philadelphia Museum of
Art. On deposit from the
Commissioners of
Fairmount Park
Catalogue no. 219 b

William Rush
(1756–1833)
The Schuylkill Chained
1825
Spanish cedar (originally
painted), length 87½″
(222.3 cm)
Philadelphia Museum of
Art. On deposit from the
Commissioners of
Fairmount Park
Catalogue no. 219 a

William Rush's allegorical figures of *The Schuylkill Freed* and *The Schuylkill Chained* were carved as pediments for the entrances of the Fairmount Waterworks millhouse. When the wood sculptures were finished in 1825, they were painted to simulate stone—probably marble—which would have been in keeping with the design of the millhouse and the neoclassical preference for stone, rather than wood sculpture. As sculpture, the figures are strangely inconsistent. They appear to be a compromise between a neoclassical ideal as seen in the classical head, attire, and graceful gesture of the female (*The Schuylkill Freed*), and a romantic desire for greater expressiveness through the movement and emotion of the male figure (*The Schuylkill Chained*). To symbolize the resistance of the ancient Schuylkill to its newly chained or "improved" state, Rush emphasized the wildness of the natural state of the river with the more rugged male figure, creating an emotional conflict between the conqueror and the conquered, and thus interpreting the Waterworks as an enslavement. The female, who is emblematic of the Waterworks, is shown as a serene conqueror whose hand guides the churning water wheel; behind her is the ascending main which pours water into an urn representing the reservoirs on top of Fairmount.

Thomas W. Mason (about 1820–1899)
Fairmount Fire Company Engine Model
About 1842–65
Wood and brass, height 12" (30.5 cm)
INA Museum, INA Corporation, Philadelphia
Catalogue no. 317

This fire engine model is a replica of the hand pumper purchased by Philadelphia's Fairmount Fire Company in 1842, that company's last piece of hand-operated equipment. Built by John Agnew, "dean" of Philadelphia engine manufacturers, the pumper shows the advanced development of the Philadelphia-style engine. The pumping brakes and platforms fold out from their compact transport position to reveal a double-deck, end-stroke engine—a style perfected by Agnew, and so efficient that it was widely adopted elsewhere. A hose was connected from the hydrant to the suction opening (the lower connection on each side of the engine), and hoses were attached at the four discharge positions, a pair on each side, to direct pressurized water at the fire. The play pipe atop the condenser case was generally reserved for contests to decide which volunteer fire company could pump water highest or farthest. This hand-drawn engine required about sixteen men to operate it. Four stood on the ground and four on the platforms; they could pump at a top speed of about a hundred strokes per minute for three-minute turns, after which a second crew would take over.

Thomas Mason's beautifully crafted model of the pumper clearly shows the gilt decoration and the painted condenser-case panels representing the figures of *The Schuylkill Chained* and *The Schuylkill Freed* executed by William Rush for the Fairmount Waterworks. On the front panel, a figure of Liberty holds a shield emblazoned with an eagle; on the rear, a second figure displays the shield of the city of Philadelphia and a banner reading "Prompt to Action," the motto of the Fairmount Fire Company.

John Archibald Woodside
(1781–1852)
*Fire Engine Panel: Lady
with Guitar*
1840–50
Oil on panel, 32⅜ x
21⅝" (82.2 x 54.9 cm)
INA Museum, INA
Corporation, Philadelphia
Catalogue no. 264

Volunteer firemen were fiercely proud of their engines and kept their apparatus in top repair. Although engines were manufactured in standard colors, each company had its equipment individually painted to conform with the emblems on its hats, capes, and belts. The company name was painted on its engine or inscribed on a brass plate, and painted and carved panels such as this one decorated the sides of the condenser case. These panels were removable, enabling the volunteers to exhibit them at parades and other special occasions or to protect them from exposure to heat and water.

This carved and painted panel is one of a pair by John Archibald Woodside, who was born in Philadelphia in 1781 and became known as one of the city's best sign and ornamental painters. He frequently decorated buckets, hats, and capes, as well as parade banners and panels, for the prized engines and hose carriages of a number of the volunteer fire companies of Philadelphia. He readily adapted his sign-painting techniques to create attractive patriotic or mythological compositions for these pieces, and the maidens from his signboards became Greek goddesses, angels, and genteel ladies. The significance of *Lady with Guitar* and its mate, which shows a woman playing the harp, is not understood, although it may allude to the idea of musical harmony. If so it seems likely that these panels would have been painted for the Harmony Fire Company rather than the Fame Fire Company, to which they have traditionally been ascribed.

Thomas Moran
(1837–1926)
*View Up the Schuylkill
from West Laurel Hill
Cemetery*
1870
Oil on canvas, 30 x 45″
(76.2 x 114.3 cm)
Private Collection
Catalogue no. 332b

Thomas Moran
(1837–1926)
*View from Pencoyd
Point, West Laurel Hill
Cemetery*
1870
Oil on canvas, 30 x 45″
(76.2 x 114.3 cm)
Private Collection
Catalogue no. 332a

In 1836 the young architect John Notman (1810–1865) laid out a rambling plan for Laurel Hill Cemetery with roads winding through the undulating grounds, which overlooked the Schuylkill and the open land on the west bank. Responding to Washington Irving's recommendation that "the grave should be surrounded by everything that might inspire tenderness and veneration for the dead, or that might win the living to virtue," the managers enhanced the architect's plan by placing on the grounds at least one specimen of every valuable tree and shrub capable of growing in Philadelphia's climate. Laurel Hill was to be more than a burial ground; it was to be an arboretum as well, and one highlighted by notable monuments, adding yet another dimension to the cemetery, that of a sculpture garden. It is small wonder that Laurel Hill became a great public attraction, eventually leading to the enforcement of strict rules of conduct for its visitors.

In 1870, a year after West Laurel Hill was founded, Thomas Moran was commissioned by John Jay Smith, founder of Laurel Hill and West Laurel Hill cemeteries, to paint these views of the cemetery and the Schuylkill. Moran took great artistic license in rendering his impression of the scenes. Considered as a pair, the two paintings show Moran's use of two traditional landscape devices—a closed view through a dark frame of foliage into the landscape beyond, and an open panoramic view to the horizon along a diagonal created by carefully controlled patterns of light and shade. Instead of being united by a similar approach, the two views allow Moran to demonstrate the full range of his landscape technique in low contrasting moods. In the *View from Pencoyd Point*, the bold, thrusting shape of the foreground tree and its bright autumnal coloring set an assertive tone. In the *View Up the Schuylkill*, the play of luminous greens and the pastel colors of the river and the distant landscape create a placid vista that invites meditative appreciation of the beauties of the sight.

Fairmount Park
First design 1858
Catalogue no. 313

Represented by:
Louis Napoleon
Rosenthal (active
1850–75) after Andrew
Palles
Plan of Fairmount Park
1859
Lithograph, 28¹³/₁₆ x
20⁵/₁₆" (73.2 x 51.6 cm)
Library of Congress,
Washington, D.C.

The Fairmount Waterworks and Laurel Hill Cemetery, two influential nineteenth-century ventures into landscape architecture, formed the nucleus of the Fairmount Park System, generally considered the largest municipal park in the world. When the Waterworks, a public utility, began operation in 1815, its site was landscaped as a formal public garden. Laurel Hill Cemetery, a private endeavor, never became an official part of the park; nonetheless, its impressive size and recognized beauty drew crowds to its undulating, carefully planted grounds, introducing Philadelphians to the English landscape style.

With the popularity of landscaped nature thus proven, the city in 1855 reserved as a public common adjacent to the Waterworks the 45-acre Lemon Hill estate, acquired eleven years earlier to protect the purity of the city water supply. The greatest expansion came after the Civil War, when over 220 acres were acquired on the west side of the river about the same time the unspoiled Wissahickon Valley was annexed in northwest Philadelphia.

Fairmount Park was officially created in 1867 by the state General Assembly. In 1858, well before the park's formation, the city held a park design competition and apparently adopted the plan of Andrew Palles, a civil engineer. His proposal concentrated primarily on the east side of the river, calling for a labyrinth of roads and paths to contrast with the formal plan of the Waterworks. Although Palles's design was not executed (presumably because of the Civil War), it indicates the eventual direction of the park's development.

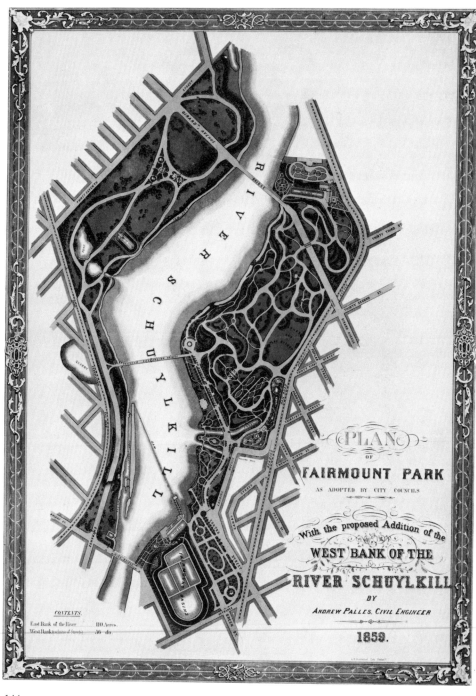

144

Hermann J.
Schwarzmann
(1846-1891) and Others
*Centennial Exhibition
Grounds and Buildings*
Parkside and
Belmont avenues
(West Fairmount Park)
1874-76
Catalogue no. 339

Represented by:
*The Centennial—Balloon
View of the Grounds*
1876
From *Supplement to
Harper's Weekly*,
September 30, 1876
Wood engraving,
20¾ x 39"
(52.7 x 76.2 cm)
The Athenaeum of
Philadelphia

On May 10, 1876, President Ulysses S. Grant and the Emperor Dom Pedro of Brazil set the giant Corliss engine in Machinery Hall into action, and the entire Centennial Exhibition in West Fairmount Park came to life. In an increasingly mechanized world, there could have been no more fitting beginning to this celebration of nineteenth-century progress.

The enormity of the fair, which might well have overwhelmed its visitors, was countered by the ingenious plan drawn up by Hermann J. Schwarzmann, which clustered exhibition buildings according to the nature of their displays in a vast triangular fairgrounds, connected by broad diagonal avenues forming long ceremonial vistas.
If the planning was innovative, the buildings were generally less imaginative. Most of the buildings

addressed the issue of architectural content, either to represent the display or make a statement about the Centennial. James H. Windrim's Agricultural Hall resembled an immense Gothic barn, Schwarzmann's Horticultural Hall, a gigantic greenhouse. The engineer of the iron and glass Main Exhibition Hall made an effort at architectural content, proposing that the building be 1876 feet in length (it came out four feet too long!). Similar symbolic content was applied to the facade of Schwarzmann's Art Gallery—the thirteen arches across the facade represent the original Colonies. This was the only exhibition building planned as a permanent structure: designated Memorial Hall, it was destined to house the Pennsylvania Museum of Art which has continued to the present day as the Philadelphia Museum of Art.

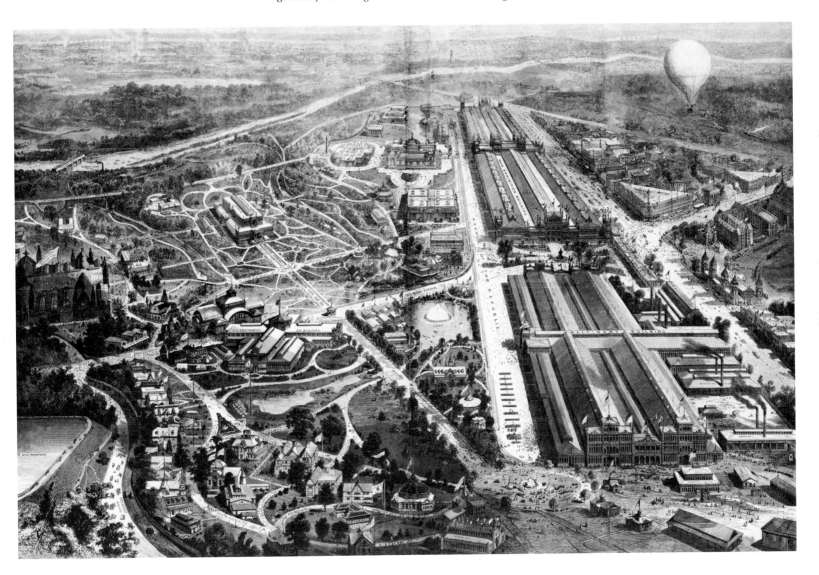

David Johnston Kennedy
(1816/17–1898)
Skating Scene (The Schuylkill River and Its Surroundings)
1864
Watercolor and gouache over pencil on paper, 9¹/₁₆ x 16¼" (23 x 41.3 cm)
Historical Society of Pennsylvania, Philadelphia
Catalogue no. 321

David J. Kennedy's hundreds of drawings of Philadelphia, executed between 1836 and his death in 1898, provide a one-man artistic survey unequaled in the city's history and almost without parallel in the United States. In many ways livelier and more revealing than the camera, Kennedy's observations encompass more than the obvious historical sites and standard picturesque views; his energetic pencil documented circuses, cigar stores, factories, lumberyards, taverns, bridges, and a variety of scenes that are charming, informative, and exceptional today precisely because they were so scrupulously ordinary then.

The view in *Skating Scene* is from the railroad embankment, visible at the lower left, on the west bank of the Schuylkill, just upstream from the Fairmount Waterworks and looking north toward

the old Girard Avenue Bridge. Fairmount Park and the Spring Garden and Northern Liberty Waterworks are seen on the far bank. The Lips Brewery buildings in the foreground and other similar sheds along the river's left bank occupy land the city was soon to purchase to enlarge the park. Several breweries with their beer gardens subsequently helped develop this stretch of the Schuylkill into a resort especially popular with Philadelphia's German community. Kennedy's spirited watercolor makes it apparent that this area was a much-frequented amusement center in winter as well as in summer.

Trotting Cracks of
Philadelphia
Published by
H. Pharazyn
1870
Lithograph with
watercolor, 23⅝ x 29⅛"
(60 x 74 cm)
The Library Company of
Philadelphia
Catalogue no. 333

These spirited horses continue to delight our eyes today as much as they did those of Victorian America. Trotting races were highly popular by the 1860s, and Philadelphians flocked to two courses, located north and south of the city. Pharazyn's superb lithograph shows a crowd of sporting enthusiasts riding home from the grandstand at Point Breeze Park, a popular racetrack in South Philadelphia, past one of the many picturesque taverns along the Philadelphia road. The anonymous artist took pains to individualize the horses and their drivers, capturing the intense expressions and skilled concentration required to manuever the straining horses past lounging and cheering onlookers on the gingerbread veranda of the hotel. In contrast to the vivid motion conjured up by the artist's rendering of churning dust, gleaming animal bodies, and whirling wheels, the background provides a relatively calm backdrop for the hectic activity in front.

Thomas Eakins
(1844–1916)
The Pair-Oared Shell
1872–76
Oil on canvas, 24 x 36"
(60.9 x 91.4 cm)
Philadelphia Museum of
Art. Thomas Eakins
Collection. 29-184-35
Catalogue no. 337

The Pair-Oared Shell shows two friends of the artist, John and Barney Biglin, practicing in their shell on the Schuylkill. Professional rowers, the Biglin brothers earned their living by competing in races throughout the country. When Eakins painted them, they had come to Philadelphia for what was probably the first pair-oared race in America. John Biglin is shown in the stroke position closer to the viewer; Barney, the younger brother, occupies the less-important bow seat. Subtle differences in position and in rendering the two rowing champions show us that it is John who sets the stroke. But the most precise treatment is reserved for the shell: all its essentials are given in sharp focus, almost as if the artist meant to explain their function by his painting. Eakins, himself an oarsman, combined his firsthand knowledge of the sport with analytical study of the scene, worked out in great detail in a series of complex preparatory drawings. The exceptional quality of Eakins's work, so distinctive from that of his contemporaries, derives in part from his thorough study and intense involvement with his subjects and his extraordinary ability to convey this personal involvement to the viewer.

Francis Speight (born 1896)
Schuylkill Valley Town
1940
Oil on canvas, 40 x 54½"
(101.6 x 138.4 cm)
Pennsylvania Academy
of the Fine Arts,
Philadelphia. Temple
Fund Purchase, 1942
Catalogue no. 476

During the thirty-six years Francis Speight spent in Philadelphia, where he taught at the Pennsylvania Academy of the Fine Arts, he was one of the most dedicated observers of the urban landscape around the city—especially the nineteenth-century industrial suburbs spreading out from the center of Philadelphia, north and west along the Schuylkill. Speight's interest in the area of Manayunk dates to his earliest years at the Academy, when he was attracted to this crowded cityscape of steep hills and ranks of row houses, each with its tiny garden. *Schuylkill Valley Town* is one of Speight's most expansive views of his favorite subject, combining a distant industrial vista with the pastoral scene in the foreground. The picture is bathed in a mellow light that blurs and softens the harsh outlines of buildings and enhances the tender spring foliage.

Despite the evident poverty of the working-class neighborhoods he so often depicted, Speight's paintings convey little of the sharp social comment characteristic of certain of his contemporaries during the 1930s and 1940s, who saw every factory or shanty as a symbol of the need for social and economic reform. Nevertheless, an exhibition of his work that perhaps made Speight happiest was held in a vacant store on Manayunk's Main Street in the 1930s and attended by the inhabitants of those very houses he loved to paint. Their pleased recognition of their own homes or a neighbor's backyard must have meant as much, if not more, to him than the impressive prizes he received in numerous exhibitions at major museums.

Edward Savage
(1761-1817)
*Action Between the
Constellation and
L'Insurgent*
1799
Aquatint and etching,
15¼ x 21¼" (38.7 x 54
cm)
American Antiquarian
Society, Worcester,
Massachusetts
Catalogue no. 150 b

Although the peace treaties that followed the Revolutionary War were signed in 1783, harassment from pirates and—with the resurgence of war in Europe—from the French warranted the building of an American navy. In 1794 the construction of three major ships was underway: the *United States,* built in Philadelphia; the *Constitution,* in Boston; and the *Constellation,* in Baltimore. These ships were constructed according to a British design, but with major improvements to increase their speed. Their first battles did not occur until 1798, when the alliance with France was terminated and orders were given to seize all French ships endangering commerce. One of the most significant naval encounters of this time occurred on February 9, 1799, when the U.S.S. *Constellation* met the French *Insurgent* in the West Indies, and within two hours, the French ship had surrendered.

Such battles provided dramatic and immediate subject matter that attracted both artists and collectors. By May 1799, Edward Savage had drawn and published two pictures of the climactic moments in this notable encounter; his are probably the first naval engravings by a native American artist, as well as the earliest aquatints produced in the United States. Here, the artist has stressed the sturdy construction and firepower of the American vessel. Although its sails are tattered, the *Constellation* is otherwise unsullied, thus emphasizing its victory; in contrast, the loser is engulfed in the smoke of cannon fire. The ship is somehow personalized and treated like a portrait of an American military hero, stressing its formidable qualities in a dramatic and courageous struggle to preserve the young nation's freedom.

William Charles
(1776-1820)
*The Cock Fight—or
Another Sting for the
Pride of John Bull*
1813
Etching with watercolor,
10½ x 14¼" (25.5 x 36
cm)
Historical Society of
Pennsylvania,
Philadelphia
Catalogue no. 187

Depictions of American naval victories became an even more popular subject during the War of 1812. Most artists, like Savage, described clear-cut scenes of battles, but others such as William Charles turned to caricature to comment on these encounters between warships. Charles's *Cock Fight* concerns the skirmish on February 24, 1813, between the American ship *Hornet* and the *Peacock*, one of the British vessels blockading the American seacoast. The *Peacock* was defeated after a gun battle of only fifteen minutes.

In Charles's version the names of the ships involved in the battle have been translated into symbols, each gaily decorated with the insignia of its country. As the hornet's sting pierces the peacock, its bedraggled tail looking much like the defeated ship's sails, King George III bemoans his loss: "Aye! What!

What! What! Brother Jonathan's Hornet killed my Peacock!!! In fifteen minutes too! Not possible. Fine Bird—well fed—I fear he was too fond of showing his tail."

A year after this encounter, a rhyme appeared suggesting that the English "Peacocks" were meeting unwonted American resistance and were thus unable to fulfill their function:
O, Johnny Bull, my joe, John, your *Peacocks* keep at
   home,
And ne'er let British seamen on a *Frolic* hither
   come,
For we've *Hornets* and we've *Wasps*, John, who as
   you doubtless know,
Carry stingers in their tails, O, Johnny Bull, my joe.

William Birch
(1755–1834)
*High Street, from the
Country Market-place
Philadelphia: with the
Procession in
Commemoration of the
Death of General George
Washington, December
26th, 1799*
From *The City of
Philadelphia,* 1800
Etching and engraving
with watercolor, 8¼ x
11¼" (20.9 x 28.6 cm)
Historical Society of
Pennsylvania,
Philadelphia
Catalogue no. 149

While Philadelphia had been recorded throughout the eighteenth century, there had been no comprehensive documentation of the city's buildings, activities, and commerce. Shortly after arriving from England in 1794, William Birch began an album of these aspects of the city, and in 1800 he published *The City of Philadelphia,* the first such systematic record in America. Birch wanted to include as many aspects of Philadelphia life as possible. Places of worship, amusement, and business; civic and cultural institutions; moments of historical significance and every-day activity; visitors and natives, artisans and merchants—all played a role in Birch's urban theater. This view of High (Market) Street includes a glimpse of the procession in commemoration of the death of George Washington that had been held on December 26, 1799. A military guard escorted the

black-draped catafalque, which was preceded by a riderless horse. The streets of the city were lined with mourners, while others crowded windows and rooftops to watch the cortege pass by. The vignette on the right of the onlooker who has turned away from the parade and weeps unashamedly into his handkerchief is one of the most moving moments in early American art.

John Lewis Krimmel
(1786–1821)
*Independence Day
Celebration in Centre
Square, Philadelphia*
1819
Watercolor with ink over
pencil on paper, 12 x 18″
(30.4 x 45.7 cm)
Historical Society of
Pennsylvania,
Philadelphia
Catalogue no. 204

John Lewis Krimmel's *Independence Day Celebration in Centre Square, Philadelphia*, depicts a boisterous gathering of soldiers and townspeople celebrating the forty-third anniversary of the Declaration of Independence in 1819. Krimmel is indebted to Birch's views of Philadelphia for his practice of showing a crowd of small figures participating in a particular outdoor event at an identifiable location. In fact, the scene in front of the Centre Square Pump House would have been recognized instantly by Krimmel's contemporaries. So, too, would the War of 1812 slogan, "Don't give up the Ship," on the naval battle poster at the left and the reference to Andrew Jackson's victory in New Orleans on a similar placard at the right. Beneath it, a woman seated at a table sells copies of the patriotic songs "Yankee Doodle" and "Hail Columbia," while one of the men behind her holds

a flyer referring to Oliver Hazard Perry's victory on Lake Erie. Next to them a small boy fires a toy pistol; another prepares to ignite a miniature cannon. A little girl runs crying to her mother, who is absorbed in the tales of an old soldier as he points to his battle scars. In the center, two soldiers evidently are boasting about the roles of their respective services in the recent war; to their left, three boys steal the wares of a woman peddler who is distracted by a lively discussion among several men gathered around an oyster stand. At the far left, a party of civilians and military men raise their glasses in a toast, to the accompaniment of a fiddler, while in the background the noise and movement continue, with marching soldiers, an officer on horseback giving orders, and a fife and drum corps.

Giuseppe Ceracchi
(1751–1801)
George Washington
1795
Marble, height 28⅞"
(73.3 cm)
The Metropolitan
Museum of Art, New
York. Bequest of John L.
Cadwalader, 1914
Catalogue no. 139

George Washington is known to have sat for only three sculptors, the Englishman Joseph Wright, the Frenchman Jean-Antoine Houdon, and the Italian Giuseppe Ceracchi. All three requested the sittings in the hope of obtaining from the United States government the commission for an equestrian statue of the president. Ceracchi first modeled a terra-cotta bust of Washington in Philadelphia in 1791/92. When the decision on the equestrian project was postponed, Ceracchi took the portrait to Europe in the summer of 1792, and from it carved a bust in marble. Later, he returned to Philadelphia, and in 1795, at his urgent request, Washington posed again so that Ceracchi could make alterations to the marble. The result was this unusual life portrait, presenting Washington in the artificial guise of a Roman emperor. Ceracchi's bust was admired by a number of his contemporaries, and praised above all for the expression of the mouth, said to be very much like Washington's. Most observers, however, were disconcerted by the cropped hair and Roman dress, which they felt disguised their hero.

154

Rembrandt Peale
(1778–1860)
George Washington
1824–60
Oil on canvas, 36 x 29"
(91.4 x 73.7 cm)
The Westmoreland
County Museum of Art,
Greensburg,
Pennsylvania
Catalogue no. 216

In the fall of 1795, George Washington agreed to sit for a portrait by Rembrandt Peale. The resulting lifelike head, one of Peale's finest achievements, became the basis for a number of his attempts to create an ideal Washington portrait. Rembrandt soon developed a plan to form a composite portrait —superior to all of the life portraits—by combining the best aspects of each. His first such portrait, painted about 1798, was primarily a copy of his father's 1795 portrait of Washington with revisions based on his own Washington portrait of the same year.

In 1823, long after Washington's death and when Gilbert Stuart's well-known likeness was being universally acclaimed as the standard representation of the first president, Rembrandt resumed his experimentation with the ideal portrait to the exclusion of nearly all else. Finally, he shut himself up in his Philadelphia studio for three months in a state of "poetic frensy" and contrived a venerable bust of Washington, afterward designated as the "porthole" portrait because it was set in an oval surrounded with simulated stonework. Rembrandt advertised this picture as "The National Portrait and Standard Likeness of Washington," which he reproduced in at least seventy painted copies. The earliest of the "porthole" type showed Washington wearing a black-velvet Roman-style mantle, but by 1824, Peale had developed an alternative version showing Washington in military uniform. This portrait is an unusually fine example of the military version, which became the type that was most frequently copied by Peale.

Osmon Reed (active
1833–63)
Presentation Ewer
1843
Silver, height 17¾"
(45 cm)
Philadelphia Museum of
Art. Purchased: Joseph E.
Temple Fund. 02-6
Catalogue no. 273

The occasion for this presentation ewer was a
successful political campaign for the Whig party in
Tennessee. The recipient was James C. Jones, who
was selected to run against James K. Polk in the
Tennessee gubernatorial race of 1841 because of his
ability to carry on a "log-cabin" campaign. Tall,
robust, and athletic, Jones was popular with the
large crowds that attended his debates with Polk,
and he won the election. In the next gubernatorial
canvass, of 1843, the Whigs again chose Jones, who
for a second time ran successfully against Polk.
Jones's victory was considered nationally significant
as a forecast of the hoped-for election of the Whig
candidate, Henry Clay, in the 1844 presidential
campaign. So important was this election considered
that the Whig party of Philadelphia presented this
ewer to Jones "as a token of their admiration of his
lofty eloquence and gratitude for his gallant services

in the Gubernatorial canvass of 1843, which
resulted in the establishment of Whig principles and
opened the Presidential campaign with sure
harbingers of the triumphant election of Henry Clay
in 1844."

The ewer is a masterpiece of Philadelphia repoussé
silver, incorporating into its ornate design flowers
such as dogwood and roses, which grew in
abundance in Tennessee. A figure, presumably
Jones, is shown "stump speaking" to an enthusiastic
crowd. The banner, held by an eagle, reading *Post
Praelia Praemia* ("After the Battle Come Rewards")
confidently predicts a victory for Clay—which never
came to pass.

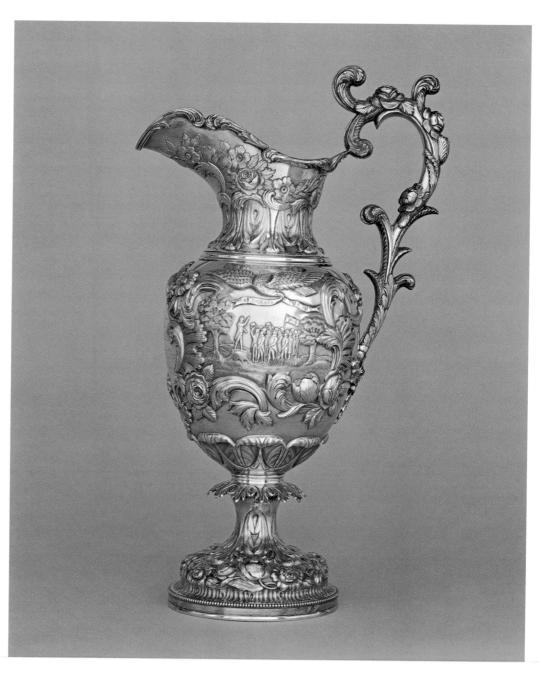

Attributed to William
Rush (1756-1833)
Eagle
About 1810-20
Painted pine, height
24¾" (62.8 cm)
Philadelphia Museum of
Art. Given by Thomas A.
Andrews. 89-35
Catalogue no. 199

The acceptance of the design for the Great Seal of
the United States in 1782 formally introduced the
eagle into American iconography, and as the
republic grew so did the use of the eagle. Early
representations included this emblem in other
political contexts, among them designs for state
shields and campaign buttons, and by 1810 the eagle
was the universal symbol of the American spirit,
appearing on items associated with military
organizations and volunteer fire companies as well
as on bottles, buttermolds, and a multitude of
other objects.

This eagle is one of several in Philadelphia
attributed to William Rush. Although none is signed
and there is documentation for only one eagle—that
made by Rush for the Pennsylvania Academy of the
Fine Arts—the style and sophistication of these pine
carvings indicate that no other Philadelphia artist,
and probably no other wood-carver in the young
nation, would have been capable of executing
such work.

Index of Artists and Makers

Photographs by Will Brown
except pages 16, 17, 28, 51, 58, 60-62, 64, 65, 86, 90, 91,
126, 129, 148 by A. J. Wyatt, Staff Photographer,
Philadelphia Museum of Art
page 22 by Conservation Department,
Philadelphia Museum of Art
pages 30, 127, 140, 141 by Charles P. Mills & Son
page 52 by Peter Lester
page 53 courtesy A.C.A. Galleries
page 59 by Geoffrey Clements
page 69 by George Fistrovich
page 98 by Greg Heins
page 111 by Richard Aufenger
page 128 by Mark Cohn
page 137 by Helga Photo Studio
pages 12, 13, 21, 29, 46, 48, 49, 56, 57, 63, 66, 67, 84,
92, 93, 99, 100, 103, 106-108, 114, 119, 135, 144,
145, 149, 154, and 155 courtesy lenders

Designed by Laurence Channing
Printed by Lebanon Valley Offset Company,
Annville, Pennsylvania